Germaine Greer

Lysistrata –

the sex strike

after Aristophanes

adapted for performance
with additional dialogue
by Phil Willmott

AURORA METRO PRESS

Founded in 1989 to publish and promote new writing, the press has specialised in new drama and fiction, winning recognition and awards from the industry.

new drama
Eastern Promise, *7 plays from central and eastern europe* eds. Sian Evans and Cheryl Robson
ISBN 0-9515877-9-X £11.99

Best of the Fest. new plays celebrating 10 years of London New Play Festival ed. Phil Setren
ISBN 0-9515877-8-1 £12.99

Young Blood, five plays for young performers.
ed. Sally Goldsworthy **ISBN 0-9515877-6-5 £9.95**

Six plays by Black and Asian women.
ed. Kadija George **ISBN 0-9515877-2-2 £7.50**

Seven plays by women, female voices, fighting lives.
ed. Cheryl Robson **ISBN 0-9515877-1-4 £5.95**

A touch of the Dutch: plays by women.
ed. Cheryl Robson **ISBN 0-9515877-7-3 £9.95**

Mediterranean plays by women.
ed. Marion Baraitser **ISBN 0-9515877-3-0 £9.95**

other
How Maxine learned to love her legs *and other tales of growing up.* ed. Sarah Le Fanu
ISBN 0-9515877-4-9 £8.95

The Women Writers Handbook eds. Robson, Georgeson, Beck. **ISBN 0-9515877-0-6 £4.95**

www.netcomuk.co.uk/~ampress

Trade distribution:

UK - Central Books Tel: 0181 986 4854 Fax: 0181 533 5821

USA - Theatre Communications Group, N.Y. Tel: 212 697 5230

Canada - Canada Playwrights Press Tel: 416 703 0201

ISBN 0-9536757-0-X Printed by Antony Rowe, Chippenham.

Germaine Greer

Lysistrata - the sex strike

After Aristophanes

Adapted for performance with additional dialogue
by Phil Willmott.

First produced in July 1999 by BAC in association with
The Steam Industry at Battersea Arts Centre, London
with the following cast and crew:

Director	**Phil Willmott**
Designers	**Rupert Tebb and Andri Korniotis**
Lighting	**Hansjorg Schmidt**
Choreography	**Faith Simpson**
Assistant Director	**Abigail Anderson**
Production and stage management:	**Lisa Mead, Rob Kinsman, Rebecca Maltby, Emma Barron, Donna Maloney, Ursula Jordon**

CHARACTERS

(Society Women)

Lysistrata *Leader of Women for Peace*

Rose Wadham

Kalonike *Lysistrata's neighbour* **Libby Machin**

Myrrhine *Leader of the Anagyrus women*

Mirren Delaney

Kalike *A young Athenian woman* **Polly Nayler**

Lampito *Leader of the Spartan women*

Amanda Osborne

Iris *Leader of the Boetian women* **Lucie Barât**

Praxagora *Leader of the Corinthian women*

Rona Sentinar

(Cleaning Women)

Stratyllis	**Amanda Symonds**
Rhodippe	**Jennie Dent**
Nikodike	**Apple Brook**
Katina *Younger*	**Patricia Jones**

(Athenian Men)

Phylurgus *An Athenian magistrate*   **William Maxwell**
Demostratus *A young Athenian public orator*
                                         Jack Mytton
Nikias *Athenian senator for finance*
                                       Alexander John
Peisander *Senator for law and order*
                                       Peter Nolan
Kinesias *An officer. Husband of Myrrhine*
                                       Nick Tizzard
A Masseur / Doorman   **Doug Duncan**

(Spartan Men)

The Spartan Herald	**Will Chitty**
The Spartan Ambassador	**Martin Hearn**

(Secret Police)
In Act One Kinesias, the doorman and the two Spartans
double as 4 Athenian Secret policemen guarding the
Senators: Theorus, Nicarchus, Dikaiopolis and Amphitheus

SETTING A bathhouse

A Guide to Production Performance style.

The characters in this adaptation of Aristophanes/Greer's text are best played as archetypes and in the broad style of classic British *Carry On* films such as *Carry On Cleo*. The cleaning women are the exception and should be played more natur- alistically. They are the emotional heart of the piece. Lysistrata's address to the women of Athens and her duo- logue with Demostratus are sincere but as a general rule if the piece is played for laughs then the politics take care of themselves.

The Set

The set should be designed in a cartoon style and represents a once grand, now dilapidated steam room adorned with male statuary and Greek columns. The whole building looks as if it has been bombed and there is a gaping hole in the back wall through which we can see The Acropolis represented as a little model on a hill. There are four benches where patrons can sit in the steam or lie to be massaged. In the centre of the back wall there is an imposing doorway with the sign:*'The Acropolis Bath House'* above it. To one side is another smaller sign: *'Male Members Only'*. To either side of the doorway are sunken pools of water. This doorway leads to other rooms in the bathhouse. Entrance to the bathhouse is through the centre of the audience and actors should be able to move freely into the auditorium. There are two trap doors in either side of the stage.

Costumes and props

In keeping with the setting of a steam room the characters spend most of the evening wearing towels. The effect of this is (a) to look sexy or ridiculous, depending on character, and (b) to give a timeless 'toga' look. The towels are colour-coded to help the audience understand who's who. The Senators wear deep burgundy-coloured towels, the cleaning women are in pink, the policemen in black, Athenian soldiers in bottle green and the Spartans in dark blue. The older men also wear smaller towels loosely around their necks to give them status. The outdoor clothes that we do see are in period but as the designers of the *Carry On* films might have viewed Ancient Greece. So the Society Women are terribly glamorous, the cleaning women, though not too ridiculous, are 'Mrs Mops'.

Phalli.

The men's erect phalli are covered by towels and only slightly larger than life, rather than ridiculous. This ensures that, whilst comic, they remain believable and desirable. The Spartan Ambassador's phallus is bigger then everyone else's, much to his delight and the other men's annoyance. Phalli should only be in evidence where specified. Using them right from the beginning will reduce their comic impact.

Group Reactions.

For most of the play there are large groups of people on stage and the response of the group to the central dialogue is very important. In rehearsals the actors should be encouraged to vocalise these reactions according to their individual characters. A guide to group reactions is included in this text. These ad-libs should be set by the director for performance and are a vital ingredient in presenting the play as a lively debate.

The Cleaning Women

The cleaning women should all have accents, each can be different, from any country or region. The performers playing these roles should adapt their lines to suit the speech patterns, vocabulary and slang of the accent they have chosen. The dialogue in this script is notated as performed by the original cast. Stratyllis had a London accent, Rhodippe and Nikodike were from Yorkshire and Lancashire and Katina was from Newcastle.

Phil Willmott.

ACT ONE

As the audience enter, 1950's dance music can be heard but thinly, as if played on a tinny old record player. Against this there are occasional loud explosions and bursts of machine-gun fire.

The dimly-lit steam room is strewn with male debris; there are piles of abandoned towels lying around, empty bottles of scotch and discarded copies of the Times-like newspaper, 'The Hoi Polloi', mocked up in a cartoon style so that every headline mentions the word 'war'. e.g. 'WAR CONTINUES', 'MORE WAR', 'WAR INTERRUPTS SPORT', 'WAR FASHION EXTRA' etc.

In the middle of all this sits a particularly fat and greasy senator being massaged. As the play starts the senator and masseur leave.

Music. (The introduction to Julie London's recording of 'Our Time Will Come' cross fades with the pre-set sound). On the lyric 'Our time will come' Stratyllis, Rhoddipe and Nikodike enter through the centre door and stand for a moment looking at the mess. They are the bathhouse cleaners.

Stratyllis is their natural leader, mouthy, inquisitive and hungry for a better life. Rhodippe is softer and more trusting, Nikodike is sharp and cynical. Their tough life has made them world-weary and cynical but they are capable of great warmth and high spirits.

They begin to clean up the mess and scrub the place clean. After a few moments Lysistrata enters. She is expecting other society women to be there. It is important that she takes no notice of the cleaning women. It is as though they are invisible. When she

removes her cloak she simply holds it out expecting someone to take it from her – and they do.
She is strikingly beautiful and very self-possessed in a plucky 'head gal' kind of way. The cleaning women carry on cleaning around Lysistrata as the music fades under her speech.

Lysistrata   Nobody here. Nearly dawn and there's nobody here. If I'd asked them to a wine-tasting or a gambling party, or a fashion show they'd have been here hours ago. But to a secret political meeting, a small matter of life and death and the future of civilisation – Oh, that's not a pressing matter. They just might drift by eventually, if nothing more urgent or interesting comes up.

Her neighbour Kalonike, a bustling big woman with an infectious dirty laugh calls to her from the back of the auditorium and makes her way to the stage.

Kalonike   Who-ooh! Hello darling!
Lysistrata   Oh Kalonike, bless you! *(They kiss)*
Kalonike   Sorry I'm late, darling. I couldn't decide which earrings to wear. Well, isn't this exciting. Come now… clear that brow, before those creases get permanent. *(She looks around)* So this is what it's like in here. I've always wondered.

She picks up a discarded male jock-strap and laughs lustfully. One of the cleaning women relieves her of it and her cloak – again barely acknowledged.

Lysistrata	This is it. The bathhouse. This is where our menfolk come to escape from women and take decisions on our behalf. The perfect place, wouldn't you say, for the first meeting of 'Women for Peace'? But where is everyone?... We're always being told that we've got no brains, that we're irresponsible and flighty. I do women the courtesy of treating them like adults and they can't even be bothered to make an appearance.

Kalonike isn't really listening, she's having a good nose around. She looks into one of the pools.

Kalonike	Ohh look darling they've got goldfish in here *(to the fish)* Hello, hello!
Lysistrata	I begin to think my father was right about women after all.
Kalonike	Well how many women are there who give a damn about foreign affairs?
Lysistrata	This isn't a foreign affair. It's a war that's ruining our lives right here and now! What could be closer to home? I bet they're still lounging in bed.
Kalonike	Darling, it is the middle of the night. You might be able to come and go as you please but other women have responsibilities.
Lysistrata	What are servants for if women can't take their minds off running the house for five minutes? This meeting is important.
Kalonike	A smoothly-run household is important too. And you keep making such a mystery about your important business that

they have no chance to judge for themselves. Can anything be so important?

Lysistrata   Indeed it is. Something I've been
sweating over during many a long
sleepless night.

Kalonike *(lustfully)* Send him round to me, love. I
know I could do with a good sweat.
(She laughs dirtily.)

Lysistrata   Could you just stop thinking about sex
for a moment? There's a lot at stake
here. We must be strong – this is our
destiny.

Kalonike   You've had a vision! How exciting. I
had one recently, did I tell you? I
dreamt I was pinned to this rock by
this great brute of a swan and he kept
arching his long muscular neck and all
my clothes fell off. What could it
mean?.. Then there's another one in
which I'm chased up a greasy column
by a boa constrictor –

Lysistrata   Kalonike! Please concentrate. All the
hopes of Greece are pinned on us
women. If only the Peleponnesians
would stop being so...

Kalonike   I just wish they'd all stop being.

Lysistrata   Why, for goodness sake? What have
they ever done to you?

Kalonike   Darling, we are at war with the
Peleponnesians.

Lysistrata   I'm not. Who's *we*? I suppose you'd
like the Boetians wiped out too?

Kalonike   Well...

Lysistrata   We can't go on like this. If the women
would only come, the Boetians, the
Peloponnesians, the women of all the

	states, we could save the whole federation between us.
Kalonike	But what can we do? All we've ever learnt to do is sit around looking ornamental.
Lysistrata	That's our strategy. Our instruments will be transparent dresses and dainty little shoes, rouge and musk.
Kalonike	How are we going to use them?
Lysistrata	In such a way that men shall never in our time lift their weapons against each other.
Kalonike	Well if it means a few more fellas lift their weapons in my direction – I'll paint my nipples gold. *(Dirty laugh. Lysistrata glares at her and the laugh withers)* Oh, isn't that?... Oh look Lysistrata. Yoo hoo! Girls!

(Myrrhine and Kalike enter through the audience. They are both young, glamorous and beautiful. Myrrhine is dizzy with the excitement of it all. Kalike is rather more nervy. As they approach the stage Lysistrata calls:)

Lysistrata	Jolly good show. Where are you two from?
Myrrhine	We're the Anagyrus girls.
Lysistrata	Ah, yes, Suburban Women's Association of Mothers for Peace, isn't it?
Myrrhine	That's right. SWAMP for short.
Kalike *(looking about her)*	Are we too late? Is it all over?

(The cleaning women take their cloaks.)

Lysistrata	I'm sorry that you couldn't make the effort to be here on time. It was rather important.

Myrrhine	I'm frightfully sorry but I couldn't find my knickers in the dark. *(She giggles with Kalike)* Well, come on then, tell us what's going on.
Lysistrata	No, no let's wait for the others to get here. The enemy women haven't arrived yet. *(The others are appalled.)* *(Trying to calm them)* I need a women's representative from every side in the war.
Kalonike	Darling this is dangerous. You've gone too far this time.

(Then from the back of the theatre we hear the approach of Lampito, Praxagora and Iris. They have darker cloaks than the Athenian women. They jog in, Lampito leading the others in a call and response chant like a US army drill sergeant.)

Lampito	Spartan girls are fit and tough,
Prax/Iris	Spartan girls are fit and tough,
Lampito	We can take it hard and rough,
Prax/Iris	We can take it hard and rough,
Lampito	We've got brains and we've got guns,
Prax/Iris	We've got brains and we've got guns,
Lampito	We're Peloponnesians.
Prax/Iris	We're Peloponnesians.

(Enter Lampito, Praxagora and Iris.)

Lysistrata	Dear Lampito, it is good to see you. How fit you look!

(Lampito elaborately warms down, showing off her physical prowess. The cleaning women take the newcomers' cloaks)

Lysistrata	What a woman. Just feel this arm. I bet you could throw a bull!

Lampito	Oh lor', Lysistrata, you are a wet! Get your tiny paw round this!

(She plants Lysistrata's hand on her breast. Lysistrata embarrassed, withdraws it.)

Lysistrata	Yes, thank you, Lampito, very impressive.
Lampito	This natty lady is Iris from Boetia.
Lysistrata	Thank you for coming so far.
Iris	Boetian women are very interested to hear what you have to say.
Lysistrata	Splendid. *(Kalonike and Myrrhine snigger to themselves at this enemy woman. Lysistrata tries to encourage them to be more welcoming)* Lovely Boetia, I always think, so neat and well kept.
Kalonike	Is it true you remove all the hairs off your legs one by one?
Iris	No, but we do pluck our pussies.
Kalonike *(somewhat taken aback)*	Oh. Goodness me.
Lysistrata	And who are you, my dear, and where do you come from?
Lampito	This is Praxagora. A nice open lass from Corinth.
Kalonike *(aside to Myrrhine)*	Have you ever met a lass from Corinth who wasn't positively gaping? *(Dirty laugh)*
Praxagora	A bathhouse in the middle of the night – an odd time and place for a meeting.
Kalike	Yes, why all this mystery?
Lampito	Yes, now that we're all here, old girl... tell us what we're here for.
Lysistrata	Well...
Myrrhine	Oh come on, what is this important business?
Lysistrata	I'll tell you but first I want to ask you a question. Don't you miss your

menfolk, always away on active service? *(The women all sigh longingly in unison)* Why, there's not one of us here that has not got menfolk away at the wars.

Kalike Do you have to ask?

Kalonike My husband's been gone five months... *(The women make sympathetic noises. These responses build in intensity and volume as each woman adds her piece)* ...messing about in Thrace, and I'm not even allowed to ask him what he's doing there.

Myrrhine My boo boo's been stationed at Pylus for the last seven months, three weeks, four days, twelve hours and thirty three and a half minutes.
(Sympathy)

Kalike My honoured spouse only comes home to accept a new medal and he's gone again.
(More sympathy)

Praxagora And it's not as if you can find a substitute. Lovers these days are harder to come by than husbands.
(Enthusiastic agreement)

Iris Even a modest eight-inch dildo has been requisitioned for war materials.
(Shocked silence. Beat. Then all at the same time, the women turn away embarrassed.)

Lysistrata Why should you put up with it any longer? If I know a way to end the war, will you help me do it?
(Enthusiasm from the women)

Myrrhine	*(leaping up and putting her hand in the air like a schoolgirl)* I know a way, I know a way. We could have parties to raise money for the cause, the most marvellous parties, and invite simply everyone. We can have the first one at my house.
Praxagora	We'll make red wine punch.
Iris	Ooh and I can make those little cheesy balls rolled in nuts, they're simply delicious.
Myrrhine	What a smashing idea!
Kalonike	I know! I'll set up a street stall and sell kisses! We can take turns standing there with hearts and frills all around... we should raise quite a lot.
Lampito	I've been meaning for a long time now to set up some women's wrestling contests. My girls and I against all comers.
Lysistrata	Very well then. Seeing as I am assured of your support, I shall divulge my plan. *(She takes a deep breath and gathers them around her. The women are on tenterhooks)* Sisters, I want you to gather together the women of all your communities and convince them that until further notice they must all agree to give up the pe – to give up the pe –...to have nothing more to do with the co –... *(frustrated at her prudishness)* Oh for heaven sake. This is the plan. It's very straightforward. Until our men see sense we simply refuse to fuck. *(The women are appalled).* Myrrhine, you've gone pale! Won't you do it? Will you all go back on your word?

Myrrhine	I can't. Not me. The war will have to go on.
Praxagora	Oh, I couldn't either.
Kalike	I liked the party plan better.
Iris	Let's just make some cheesy balls.
Kalonike	Why don't we adopt my kissing plan?
Lysistrata	Of course, you're all dead eager to snog total strangers in the street. But we're not doing fundraising. We have our funds. *(The other women are interested but confused)* Two hours ago I led a gang of women who broke into the treasury. It was easy with all the men away. Women are now in complete control of our nation's purse strings. *(They are impressed)* There is another army of women standing by to march on the Acropolis at dawn and seize the debating chamber. *(They applaud)* But it's not enough. When our men come home on leave we need to convince them that this war is futile. Withhold sex and you'll have their full attention.
	(There is an outbreak of protestations)
Women	But Lysistrata… etc
Lysistrata	Sshh! You see, it works a little bit like an economic sanction. *(They sound bored)* Oh all right, basically it's blackmail. *(Suddenly they're interested)* We let them know we've got what they want. *(As she talks they all get caught up in her sexy vision)* Drape ourselves round the house, all tarted up, little pubes all nicely plucked, titties peeping out, smelling of musk, till our men can't contain

themselves any longer. When we've got them right on the brink, trembling on the bedroom threshold, then we make our terms. *(They are brought back sharply to reality)* At first they won't think we're serious, but we will have to convince them by our perseverance that we are and that we expect our terms to be honoured. Peace in return for sex; no peace, no sex.

Lampito   You know, they say that when Menelaus went to execute Helen for causing a ten-years war, she just let him see her boobs and he threw his sword away.

(They all check their own cleavage hopefully but sigh and give up as Iris says:)

Iris   That'll only work if you've got tits that would launch a thousand ships.

Praxagora   But why should our husbands put up with it? What if they just walk out?

Lysistrata   Well, you'll just have to survive until they come back, won't you? There are other things you can do, you know. Necessity is the mother of invention.

Myrrhine   Proverbs won't keep me warm in bed.

Lampito   Would you like me to come around and keep you warm, dear?

(The women all laugh warmly as Lampito puts her arm round Myrrhine. Myrrhine looks slightly nervous)

Praxagora   But what if they use force?

Iris   What if they knock us about?

Lampito   Well, we'll just have to give them a good kick in the rising passion won't we?

Kalonike *(genuinely worried)* And what about afterwards? I don't want my head knocked off.

Lysistrata	If you have to have sex, give in as grudgingly as possible. Make sure he doesn't enjoy it. Lie like a dead woman and sigh every now and then, tell them they've only got a little one or something like that. *(Uproarious laughter)*
Kalonike	You're very bright, Lysistrata, much brighter than me.

(She waits for everyone to correct her. They do not.
Then they realise and hurriedly do so. She is placated)

Kalonike	If you think it's the only way, I'll go along with you.

(They let out girly screams of joy and sing the special
playground clapping game they have played as a sign
of their friendship since childhood:)

Women	Under the bramble bushes, Under the sea, Boom, boom, boom... *(More girly giggling)*
Lampito	Spartan husbands are simple souls. An erect cock will agree to anything. I'm in! *(She and Lysistrata do a high five)* But your Athenian men with their platonic love, your sexual sophisticates, I doubt you'll get the better of them so easily.
Lysistrata	Don't worry Lampito, we can handle them.
Kalike	What will you do about this emergency government?
Iris	What's it called? The Committee of Public Safety or something?
Lysistrata	The Probuli.
Praxagora	They're not going to be very happy when they arrive at the Acropolis tomorrow to find it full of women.

Lysistrata	Oh, they're nothing to be afraid of. A cluster of old blimps, too old to serve in this war, bumbling round the city trying to maintain law and order. They spend more time hiding in this bathhouse then they do on achieving anything.
Lampito	But they are protected by four secret police. You are under virtual martial law here and the old men have all the power.
Lysistrata	We're using that to our advantage. The women who are attacking the Acropolis have disguised themselves as war veterans making a sacrifice to the gods of war. You should see them – my aunt's got herself up as the most fearsome warhorse, bristling with whiskers. The few guards that there are won't dream of barring the way. Then once the women are inside, it's ours.
Kalonike	Oh, that explains the terrifying creature that came out of Minnie's house this morning – it must have been her in disguise. I thought she'd got a soldier round to give her a bit of basic training. *(Dirty laugh)*
Lampito	You've thought everything through, haven't you? I don't know why you needed to consult us.
Lysistrata	Because… unless the women of all sides try to convince the men to declare peace, all of this will be wasted. We have something they want and we can bargain with it. By seizing power within the bedroom we can

	force the men to ratify our proposals for ending the war. *(They applaud)*
Iris	Whew! You've really bitten off something big.
Praxagora	I haven't had something that big in my mouth for a long time.
Kalonike	I vote we suck it and see. *(Dirty laughter)*
Kalike	We can't afford to fail, you realise. They'll say we committed a treason against democracy.
Lampito	Well, I'm sure my gals are all prepared for a stretch in a women's prison.

(Kalonike laughs but Lysistrata quietens them all down and goes to comfort Kalike)

Lysistrata	I promise you darling, it will never come to that.
Kalike	I'm sorry, darling. I'm just being silly.
Lysistrata	Good girl! Now that you know the full extent of our commitment, are you ready to swear the solemn oath of solidarity?
All	Yes!
Lysistrata	We don't want to leave any incriminating documents lying about. So I suggest we simply swear.
Kalonike	We need to solemnise it though. How do we do that? *(They think hard)*
Myrrhine	Did anybody see the *Seven Against Thebes? (Murmurs of appreciation for such a wonderful show)* There was a smashing oathtaking in that.
Praxagora	I saw that! They slaughtered a sheep.
Kalike	Ooh yes! And then they poured its blood into an upturned shield and mixed it with the brains, intestines,

honey and wine and drank it, didn't they? *(Everyone looks sick)*

Lampito They pretended to.

Lysistrata Oh no, that's the sort of barbarous nonsense the warmongers go in for. We've got to have a peace ritual.

Lampito What about ripping the head off a goat, or if we ate the heart of a bull?

(Lysistrata exits upstage centre)

Kalonike Too messy. Hey! What about eating those hallucinogenic mushrooms? What is it the Dionysians are into?

Lampito Usually paranoia by daybreak.

Iris *(hippy)* Why don't we centre ourselves and meditate?

(Lysistrata enters with wine in a bowl)

Lysistrata No, we've got to pledge it by an outward sign. I suggest we simply drink to our success.

Kalonike I know I could do with a stiff one. *(Dirty laugh)*

Lysistrata *Kalonike!* This is deadly serious. *(She stamps her foot angrily and Kalonike sulks)* Now sisters, hold hands.

(They all join hands in a semi-circle. Kalonike, still sulking is on the end)

Praxagora Ooh! It smells like nectar.

Iris Where did you get it? Ooh, that reminds me, Agreeta says they've got a special offer on down at –

Lysistrata Will you all please pay *attention!* Just for a moment longer. We've got to make our pledge. Kalonike, *(Kalonike looks at her witheringly)* you lead the others in repeating the words of the oath after me. *(Kalonike is so thrilled she stops sulking and pushes into the semi-circle beside Lysistrata)* The rest of you hum, right? *(Lampito does a complex and showy warm-up)*

Lysistrata Ready?

(Lampito joins the group)

1,2,3… *(They begin to hum)*

All OMMMMM

Lysistrata I will not open my legs for husband or lover…

(Myrrhine lets out a squeal of excitement)

Kalonike *(feebly)* I will not open my legs for husband or lover…

Lysistrata Though he comes to me hard and hurting with desire…

(Kalike shudders with desire on the word 'hard')

Kalonike *(breaking out of the circle)* Oh, Lysistrata, I'm trembling all over! I've gone weak at the knees!

(They stop humming in irritation at this interruption)

Lampito *(sternly)* Though he come to me hard and hurting with desire…

(The women resume humming with renewed intensity, prompting Kalonike back to the circle. As the oath continues, all the women get more and more turned on)

Lysistrata I shall display myself before him in languid attitudes…

Kalonike I shall display myself before him in languid attitudes…

Lysistrata Disport my polished limbs to provoke his lust…

Kalonike Disport my polished limbs to provoke his lust…

Lysistrata	In saffron silk as thin as mist and all the spices of the Orient...
Kalonike	In saffron silk as thin as mist and all the spices of the Orient...
Lysistrata	But he shall be so enticed only to be denied my love...
Kalonike	But he shall be so enticed only to be denied my love...
Lysistrata	If in his masculine rage he should try to force me...

(Myrrhine and Kalike begin to pant with desire)

Kalonike *(her voice breaking)* If in his masculine rage he should try to force me...

Lysistrata	I shall go rigid and think of Greece.
Kalonike	I shall go rigid and think of Greece.
Lysistrata	I shall not wave my feet above my head...
Kalonike	I shall not wave my feet above my head...
Lysistrata	Nor point my bottom in the air like the cat in the carving.
Kalonike	Nor point my bottom in the air like the cat in the carving.

(Everyone is completely carried away by this point, panting and moaning and building to orgasm)

Lysistrata	If I am sincere in this oath let me drink from this bowl...
Kalonike	If I am sincere in this oath let me drink from this bowl...
Lysistrata	If not, let the wine turn to water in my mouth.

(They all scream, 'climaxing' together and collapse in a heap on the floor, panting. Suddenly they all lunge for the wine but Lysistrata gets there first)

Lysistrata   You have all sworn?

All *(frustratedly)* Yes!

Lysistrata   Then thus I sacrifice the victim.
(She drinks deeply)

Kalonike   Hey, remember we've all got to get some! Here's to us, the saviours of our country and the world!

(They cheer. Kalonike passes the bowl around the group. They all take a drink)

Lampito   Right-ho dear. I'm off to get the message home. Spartan women are used to organising, so I expect it'll go swimmingly. Don't worry about a thing.

(The cleaning women begin to help the society women on with their cloaks)

Lysistrata   Good luck, all of you. Let us know how you get on. I propose that this bathhouse becomes our headquarters. We will find our strength and sanctuary as the men have always done. But from now on the talk here will be of peace not war.

Kalonike   But the four secret police, won't they rush in and overpower us?

Lysistrata   We'll have to organise for resistance and train. We'll get all women to come to a conference here. Lampito, you can lead self-defence classes and martial arts and – er– blandishment training.

Kalonike   What about belly-dancing classes?

Kalike   Health and beauty regimes?

Praxagora   Massage?

Iris   Fashion shows?

Lysistrata   Whatever we like. The treasury is taken. In a few hours the Acropolis will fall to us and tomorrow we make this bathhouse our own. *(They cheer)* What are you waiting for ladies? Chop, chop.

The sun's almost rising. You've got to
spread the word. No peace –

All   No sex !

*(All exit through the audience, except Kalonike who is
fetching her handbag)*

Kalonike *(to herself)* I can't even manage to diet. How
can I change the world? I can't even
change myself. I wish my husband
wanted to see me in see-through
dresses. Wanted me. *(She swaddles
herself in her cloak and trots off after
them)* Hey, darlings! Wait for me!

*(The three cleaning women: Nikodike, Stratyllis and
Rhodippe, move downstage into the light.)*

Nikodike   What a lot of bollocks! *(She and Rhodippe go straight for the wine bowl
while Stratyllis stands apart, lost in
thought.)* What do them women know
about war? What have they ever been
through?

Rhodippe   That one who got them all together...
what's her name, Lysistrata? She
doesn't know she's born. Never even
had any kids.

Nikodike   All sleek and well fed, they've got time
to sit around hatching up plans for
saving the world. Greek civilisation,
what's it ever meant to us?

Rhodippe   Oh but wouldn't it be fun though, to sit
around in our flimsy whimsies and
waggle our arses at our lord and
master? *(she waggles her bottom)*

Nikodike	I wonder whose hard work went into making this wine she's been hoarding. Bit of a tippler she is an' all, I'd say.
Rhodippe	What about that Amorgos silk she wants to doll herself up in? That work's so fine, the weavers go blind. They use kids on the looms too. Fat lot she cares.
Stratyllis	I think she might have something.
Nikodike	How could she? Her husband's coming home. I bet he never even saw no fighting. It's our lads do all the dirty work.
Stratyllis	Yeah, love, I know. But what other hope have we got? She's bright, energetic, rich. All that means she's got power. She's a looker too, that's more power. I bet she can even read.

(Katina, a pale-faced young woman, in threadbare black clothes and carrying a bundle wrapped in cloth enters from the audience, sobbing. As she arrives on the stage, she trips and her bundle scatters its contents over the stage.)

Nikodike	Nay, love, don't cry like that! You'll set us all off!
Rhodippe *(picks up the tiny clothes from her bundle)*	Look at this.
Katina	Do you like them? *(handing out clothes to Stratyllis and Nikodike like an eager street vendor)* My mother-in-law did them. I was hoping to sell them.
Nikodike	Sell 'em? Who to, for heaven's sake?
Katina	Anybody who'll give me food, or money for food.
Rhodippe	Nobody's buying baby clothes, luv. No one's seen a man long enough to make babies in months. Years in some

cases. And we don't know *if* let alone *when* we'll ever see them again. And we've no money any road.

Katina I thought some of the richer women perhaps...

Rhodippe *(shaking her head)* You're from the mountains aren't you?

Katina Thessaly. Foreign soldiers came one day, took our animals and torched our crops. Then the national army came and took my father-in-law, my husband and my brother away somewhere, to fight the foreigner soldiers. I didn't begrudge them. I was proud to see them go.

Stratyllis Why didn't you begrudge them?

Katina *(shocked)* They were fighting for me, for my country!

Stratyllis They were fighting a crappy war in Sicily. All over a shitty little colony that nobody's ever given a toss about. That's what our men are dying for.

Katina My mother-in-law couldn't cope. She just sat all day in her rocking chair and stared at the wall. But after she died, I couldn't run the farm on my own, so I locked everything up and went with the others who were fleeing the fighting but no one would take us in. My baby came too early on the road... these things have never been worn.

Stratyllis This endless bloody war!

Rhodippe My old man couldn't wait to join up, daft old goat. Thought it'd be a right laff. I bet he's not laughing now.

Stratyllis	At least if that lot succeed in ending the war, we'd know whether our old men were coming back or not.
Nikodike	If I really thought that any plan for ending the war was going to work, I'd give it a try. But I don't see how this lot can get anywhere. They think all you've got to do is have a committee, go to a few fancy do's and you've changed summat. It's all so bloody daft.
Rhodippe	How on earth is cock-teasing going to put an end to the war? It won't make the men any less touchy for a start. It's just like bringing the war into your own home.
Stratyllis	I think it does make sense, and it'll teach 'em a lesson – the warmongers.
Katina	I thought only generals and that, could be warmongers.
Stratyllis	Oh no. Most of the blokes in our part of the world thought it was a big adventure. A chance to skive off working in the fields. They marched off grinning, thinking it was a little holiday – getting pissed every night and kicking a few heads in – they loved it. That's a warmonger, as far as I'm concerned. We've got to make 'em see sense.
Katina	Get involved ourselves, do you mean?

(The four Secret Police: Theorus, Nicarchus, Dikaiopolis and Amphitheus, suddenly burst in S.A.S. style with machine-guns, through the trapdoors and up through the water troughs at the back. They are all wet and wearing snorkels which they blow water out of as they arrive, then they put on their cool sunglasses and

start to check out the place for enemy action.
The elderly Senators enter from the audience.
Phylurgus is their pompous over-bearing leader.
Nikias is sly and weasle-like, Peisander an aggressive
bulldog of a man.)

Phylurgus   *Good god*! Of all the nerve. Thrown
                       out of the Acropolis by a bunch of
                       women.

Stratyllis   Looks like we *are* involved!

(The women melt back upstage out of the light)

Theorus   I don't know why you don't let us
                       secret police blast them out for you,
                       sir.

Phylurgus *(sarcastic)* Oh well, that would be
                       wonderful for troop morale, wouldn't
                       it? News from the home front: 'Trade
                       embargoes holding steady, oh, and by
                       the way we've just mown down your
                       granny at the Acropolis!'

Nikias   The older you get, the less you know
                       what the blazes to expect.

Peisander   I never heard of anything like it. No
                       one has. Where's the rest of the Probuli
                       got to? I told everyone to meet us here.

Phylurgus   Thank heavens for the bathhouse. At
                       least here we can take a breather away
                       from those harridans. Work out what
                       on earth to do. *(Angry again)* That
                       those blighted sluts we're silly enough
                       to keep and feed should sneak into the
                       Acropolis –

Peisander   Dressed as returned servicemen, hustle
                       us all out –

Nikias   And pelt us with rotten vegetables. My
                       clothes stink. It's good to get out of
                       them. I mean, it's so embarrassing!

Phylurgus   I can't understand how those silly
                     bitches got this bee in their bonnets in
                     the first place.

Peisander   Those half-wit women could never
                     have planned a coup d'état.

Theorus   Bloody dykes the lot of them sir, from
                     what I saw of 'em.

Peisander   No band of extremists, no peace freaks
                     can be allowed to interfere with the
                     due process of democracy.

Nikias   I put it down to frustration.

Nicarchus   You won't find any slim good-looking
                     girls, sir...

Phylurgus   Hah! In that raucous bunch, bags the
                     lot of 'em.

Amphitheus   That's what gets them at it you see, sir?

Dikaiopolis   All they want is a good – *(Much
                     raucous laughter in agreement)*

Peisander   Pah! Who'd be likely to give it to 'em?
                     Mouldy hags.

Phylurgus *(knowingly)* No, no. You're wrong, you
                     know. It's the menopause makes them
                     crazy like that. *(All men lean in to hear
                     his words of wisdom)* Did you know
                     that the vast majority of female crimes
                     are committed immediately prior to or
                     during... *(big build up)* menstruation.

All *(knowingly)* Ah.

*(Demostratus enters from the audience. He is younger
than the other Senators and has an eye patch covering
an injury from a past war. This gives him a rather
rough, sexy air)*

Demostratus   Your honour, I bring word from their
                     leader, Lysistrata.

(The secret police rush forward and train their guns on him)

Phylurgus *(to the police)* Oh, get out of the way.

Demostratus She wishes to discuss your surrender of power to the women.

Phylurgus Surrender! I've never heard anything like it.

Demostratus It seems all the other Senators have fled the city.

Peisander Lily-livered bunch of cowards, the lot of them.

Demostratus If we choose to remain then this woman, Lysistrata wishes to lay down conditions.

Nikias Does she indeed!

Demostratus She proposes an immediate meeting at the headquarters of 'Women For Peace'.

Phylurgus And where the blazes is that when it's at home?

Demostratus Apparently the headquarters are here your honour.

(The secret police franticly look for interloping women)

Nikias *Here!* In the bathhouse. But... but...

Peisander No! No! *(The secret police calm down a bit)* There must be some mistake lad. No woman has ever set foot in here.

Police Yeah!

Phylurgus Now see here, Demostratus, what are you going to do about this? *(The police crowd around him with their guns raised to his head)* You're a young man, a hero from the last campaign.

Police Campaign!

Phylurgus Your wounds, like mine, are a badge of honour.

Police	Honour!
Phylurgus	It was your speeches sent the lads back into battle again. Can't you talk some sense into a few over-excited females?

(The police all slap him on the back encouragingly and move away)

Nikias	Any right-minded person can see Lysistrata's guilty of every crime in the book.
Peisander	We'll hurry up the presentation of the charges.
Nicarchus	We'll take great pleasure in arresting her for you, sir.
Amphitheus	Yeah, sometime when she hasn't got those old biddies around her.
Theorus	Yeh, we could take her down the station for a bit of 'questioning'. *(All dirty laugh)* I'll be the first in the queue.

(The Police exit through the audience enthusiastically)

Demostratus	Don't do it.
Police *(stopping)*	What?
Phylurgus	Why? Whyever not?
Demostratus	I'm telling you as a public orator that if these apes are seen mistreating Lysistrata, we'll be lynched. She might talk nonsense but she's got a terrific act. A gentle patrician girl drawn from her quiet, comfortable home to lead a troupe of gentlewomen in an attempt to save the city – she's an instant myth. They'd probably make her queen or something. Propaganda is my job and I've got to tell you she's very sincere. Fortunately the sincere ones are always

the easiest to manipulate. Invite Lysistrata to send an observer to some token peace talks. It's an easy matter to arrange peace talks. And she'd soon get tired of it. Give her some tedious political chores to do – that'll soon dampen her ardour. But whatever happens it looks like you'll have to meet with her.

Phylurgus   No female will ever get the upper hand in this bathhouse.

Peisander   A woman shall be subject to a man, that's the law!

Nikias   However let it be said we were outdone by a bunch of bob-tailed bitches. God is on our side.

(Music. The Julie London song 'Must Be Catching' plays. The men all look about fearfully)

Phylurgus   What's that noise?

(In time to the music, Stratyllis, Rhodippe, Nikodike and Katina enter mock-sexily from centre stage entrance with full cleaning paraphernalia. They move to the music over the following lines whilst seeming to clean. The police are at a loss to know what to do because there's no obvious attack. The women could simply be cleaning.)

Phylurgus   Great heavens, can't you read the signs. This is 'Men Only'.

Stratyllis   Is it? We've been coming here for years. I never noticed. Did you girls?

Women   No.

(The women all 'sweep' the men upstage to sit on the benches. They swing their mop or brush up in the air,

*narrowly missing the men's heads as they execute a
nifty turn in their dance)*

Nikias   What do you mean? Women aren't
allowed here.

Stratyllis   Well, ain't that strange? We've been
coming in here every night to scrub the
place from top to bottom. If we'd
known, we wouldn't have bothered.

Peisander   Ah, you're cleaners. Well, that's
different.

Stratyllis   We thought we might give the place a
bit of a once over now actually.

Demostratus *(moves centre to try and restore calm)*
Ladies, I'm afraid this isn't a good
time. We have urgent business to
discuss.

(The women all scrub Demostratus)

Nikodike   Oh don't mind us. You just carry on as
if we weren't here.

Rhodippe   Hey, give us a snog!

Katina   You're a bit of alright aren't you,
darlin'?

Nikias   How dare you permit yourselves these
liberties!

Peisander   I demand to see some I.D.

Demostratus   We're discussing matters of national
importance. This is no place for
women. We've got work to do here.

Stratyllis   Work, Senator? Since when do the
likes of you have to work?

Demostratus   It is a matter of national security; troop
movements, top secret.

(The women slam buckets down on the Senators' toes)

Senators   *OW!*

Stratyllis   Troops, troops, troops. Is that your
solution to everything?

(The women squirt the men in the eyes with squeezy bottles)

Amphitheus	Now ladies this has gone beyond a joke. I must insist you leave.
Nikodike	Eh! We're not ladies, mate. We're bitches, like the ones you were talking about.

(The women throw water from the buckets in the men's faces, washing the detergent out of their eyes. They dry the men roughly with dusters)

Nikias	We don't want to have to get rough with you. Come on now, be sensible.
Rhodippe	What would a daft ha'peth like you know about what's sensible and what's not?
Katina	Look at him. He's the spitting image of our old billy goat.
Phylurgus	Don't you think it's a bit childish of you to stoop to vulgar insults?
Peisander	Why are we wasting words on this ignorant scum?
Stratyllis	That's us. Vulgar, ignorant scum!

(The women turn on the men and chase them upstage)

Rhodippe	And we'll be eating the likes of you to stay alive, if the war goes on.
Phylurgus	You wouldn't get much off us. We're too tough.
Katina	That's why we intend to boil you. Oh shit! I forgot me bouquet garni!
Rhodippe	It'll be shish kebab, we'll make of you, lad. Just the juicy bits, liver, thighs and tits!
Nikias	Shut up, you old cow. Come a little closer and I'll tie your tits in a love knot.
Nikodike	I'm quicker than you, I'd bite your balls off and spit out the pips.

Demostratus	Whatever became of the gentler sex?
Stratyllis	The female of the species is more deadly, they say.
Theorus	This is what happens when you don't keep them in their place, sir.

(The women turn on the soldiers, who are cowering in a group in upstage exit with their brooms held like guns)

Phylurgus	I feel I must warn you – you are going too far.

(The women advance threateningly on Phylurgus and surround him centre stage)

Nikodike	Would this be a good time to talk about war widows' pensions?
Katina	Yeh, aren't we entitled to anything? After all our misery?
Stratyllis	There's nothing in the kitty, love. They've spent it all on this bloody Sicilian campaign. Even if you had a pension, the cost of food's so high, you'd still have to steal it.
Nikodike	And there's no money for pensions any road. All the money from tax has been given over to the war effort.
Stratyllis	Some people make money out of the war.
Rhodippe	Not me, not on my mother's life.
Stratyllis	Of course not you. You've never had a penny to bless yourself.
Katina	You mean you can actually make money out of a war?
Theorus	You, darlin'? You could make money easily, if you could just get that cheeky bottom to where the troops are.
Nicarchus	Small supply meets big demand!

(The police laugh dirtily, while the Senators grab the benches and try to make a safe enclave behind them downstage)

Phylurgus   That is enough. All of you women are under arrest. Once again law-abiding citizens are subjected to yet another case of riot among the women of this city. These disturbances of the peace –

Stratyllis   Of the *what*?

Phylurgus   These disturbances of the peace cannot be allowed to continue. Your behaviour is quite incompatible with our ideal of feminine dignity. These new-fangled Dionysic cults are simply an excuse for drunkenness, drug-taking and wild music. That women should now be mixing politics in with this unruliness and immorality clearly necessitates the intervention of the forces of law and order.

(As the Senators gain in confidence they put the benches down and stand on them to make their point, getting into full rhetorical flow)

Peisander   Well said.

Phylurgus   It's small wonder that we have had so little success in the Sicilian campaign, when each of our young soldiers has been brought up in an atmosphere of indulgence and neglect.

Police   Yeah!

Nikias   The problem of juvenile delinquency has arisen because women are too busy interfering in men's business to do the noble work for which they were created...

Police   That's right!

Nikias   …as nurturers of life and first teachers
                     of our sons.
Lysistrata *(from the back of the auditorium)* Really
                     Senator? How very interesting.

*(Music. Marilyn Monroe's 'I want to be loved by you'
plays as Lysistrata and the other women appear
dressed in towels for the bathhouse and stand in a
group facing the men. They look very sexy and move to
the music. The men are totally gob-smacked and
enthralled.)*

Phylurgus *(almost apoplectic with frustration)* Look at
                     them! Look at them! Floozies! When I
                     was a lad, no decent woman would
                     dream of parading around the men's
                     bathhouse in a state of semi-nudity. It's
                     no wonder that sex crimes are on the
                     increase.
Nicarchus   The way they look at a man–
Amphitheus   And giggle at you.
Dikaiopolis   Waggling their –
Theorus   God, it's more than flesh and blood can
                     stand.
Phylurgus *(fighting against being aroused by them)*
                     And I won't stand for it. That is why I
                     propose to use my wartime powers in
                     the interests of the public good.
                     Leniency and wishy-washy decision-
                     making have done us nothing but harm.
                     Our whole way of life is under threat
                     from these unruly females. Guards!
                     (The guards raise their guns)
Demostratus   No!
Lysistrata *(unruffled)* Guns senator? I'm sure that
                     won't be necessary. Guns are not our
                     way at all.

(The sexy women move in on the guards who are so horny that they are completely unable to function)

Lysistrata   Aphrodite is our armourer and our weapons are the invincible powers of charm and tenderness.

(The women are caressing the guards who get erections, but then suddenly knee them in the balls. When they are on the ground, the girls kick them onto their stomachs and sit on their backs facing the audience. They pass the guns to other women who throw them into the plunge baths at the back. The guards are groaning through the following section)

Demostratus   Did you see that! Did you see that! I insist sir, you bring an action against these women for common assault.

Peisander   Moreover, these hags used offensive, abusive and insulting language.

Phylurgus   You are also charged with unlawful assembly leading to an affray and... and... and lots of other crimes that we haven't thought up yet. Your punishment will be harsh and brutal so that your treatment may serve as an effective deterrent.

Nikias   All civil liberties may be waived in circumstances of war.

Rhodippe   That in't fair!

Stratyllis   The first bad language we heard was from you.

Phylurgus   Silence, please.

(The women sitting on the men pick up their heads by the hair and bash them on the ground knocking them temporarily unconscious to keep them quiet)

Phylurgus   If you have any complaints I dare say that, some time in the future, we can organise an internal investigation.

(The women all groan, Senators say: 'Hear! Hear!')

Phylurgus	You will be allowed to speak or not, as the case may be.
Lysistrata	What about a public enquiry about the way you're conducting the war?
Women	Yes!
Lysistrata	We women have been having all kinds of thoughts we'd like to air in public.
Phylurgus	What on earth has got you females interested in matters of peace and war? Too much time hanging on your hands? A few months in the slammer and you'll be aching to get back to your dusters and mixing bowls.
Kalonike	You don't scare us!
Lampito	Not a bit!
Phylurgus	But who's keeping the home fires burning? Who's looking after the children while you're making whoopee in the Acropolis?
Lysistrata	Why won't you listen to us, Senator? What we have to say is for your good too. Why are you so intolerant?
Phylurgus	It irritates me, to be forced to listen to your opinionated drivel. You're a – a– do-gooder, you bossy ba – *(Stratyllis suddenly grips him in a head lock)* Aaargh!
Stratyllis	Keep a civil tongue, my old darling. You just might run your head into a wall.
Lysistrata	I think it's time you were forced to listen.

(The women are sat on the police facing the audience. They swing round to face Lysistrata. The police groan with relief as the girls get off, then groan again in pain when they sit back down on them.)

Lysistrata   All through the years of this long, dreary war, we allowed you men to act in our name. We trusted you and chose not to ask questions. As a result, we didn't know what atrocities you were inflicting every day on other women and their children. We honoured soldiers and admired their uniforms. We didn't dare to disapprove of you. But as this endless war grinds on and on, we women are not prepared to sit in the shadows any longer.
(The women all agree loudly)

Phylurgus   How sweet. And what do you women think you can possibly achieve?

Lysistrata   We have met together with our enemies *(The men are shocked)* and agreed to unite to overthrow you warmongers. We called a rally of women from all the states in the archipelago – yes, even the enemy women. And we planned our strategy. We've signed a peace treaty as women, and representatives of the largest single group in our warring countries. *(She turns to the women)* Did we meet or didn't we, with the women of the enemy?

Women   We met. *(They stand)*

Lysistrata   Did we agree to unite to overthrow the war and our warlords?

Women   We agreed.

(They each place a foot on the prostrate policemen at their feet)

Lysistrata   Will we stand firm with our sisters?

Women   We will stand firm.

(All the women do the 'Women For Peace' sign)

Nikias   You all heard that. Collaborating with the enemy. That's not going to sound very good in court.

Lysistrata   Well, why don't we find out? We could set up our own little court room here.

Phylurgus   That's fine by me. I am the Magistrate and since you've turned the Acropolis into a sewing circle, I've nothing else to do today.

Lysistrata   I don't think you quite understand. It's the women of Athens who will be sitting in judgement on you.
(The women laugh)

Phylurgus   Us? That's ridiculous. *(to the guards)* Now come on, men. Either you take control of these women or you'll be court-martialled and shot! Someone, get their names.

(The guards get up and advance menacingly on the women who were sitting on them, who scream and huddle together)

Stratyllis   Watch what you're doing, boys. Whatever you do to those girls we'll do to you. *(The guards laugh evilly and crack their knuckles, warming up for the torture)* And don't forget we know your mothers.

(The guards are suitably terrified by this, scuttle to the back and sit cross-legged like good boys)

Phylurgus   Close ranks men! Not one of you with the courage to outface this squeaking pack! *(Stratyllus gets behind him and grabs his ear)* Aargh!

Stratyllis   Behave yourself now darlin'. You're not dealing with nice girls now. If Lysistrata wants to talk to you, you can listen politely.

Police *(like polite little boys)* Politely!

Phylurgus   This is insurrection, violence!
*(Nikodike begins to advance on him
with fists held up. He runs away)* Help!
Help! Strapping brutes! What sort of
women are you?

Nikodike   Normal, you old bugger. Loved our
husbands, gave them kids, the more
fools we.

Stratyllis   So you show a little respect.

Lysistrata   We hunger and thirst for justice, and
we shall have it, whether you like it or
not. We say, put the Senators on trial.

*(The women cheer and begin to chant 'Athena!' in the
style of the studio audience for the Ricki Lake show:
'Go Ricki'. They come and sit amongst the audience.
All their reactions from the audience are reminiscent of
a Jerry Springer show audience. Two benches are
pulled together to make a 'dock'. Meanwhile all three
Senators are manhandled up onto this dock by the
cleaning women. Lots of noise from everyone.
Lysistrata silences everyone when the court is set up.)*

Demostratus   Your honour, *(as he walks across the
stage the women wolf-whistle; he
acknowledges them graciously)* if these
women claim to have a grievance, we'd
better be seen to give it a hearing. I
doubt it will make much difference to
the outcome of the case, but it is one
way justice may appear to be done in
these – er– confusing circumstances.

Peisander   It is inexcusable that they should have
taken the law into their own hands.

Demostratus   But we have nothing to lose by hearing
what they have to say. I ask you, your

honours, to go through with this. We might as well let her condemn herself out of her own mouth.

Lysistrata Senator Nikias, as wartime finance minister *(the women blow raspberries)* you are charged with misappropriation of public funds.

Nikias How dare you! Only last night your women marched into the treasury and stole the contents.

Women Athena! Athena! Athena!

Lysistrata *(silencing them)* We didn't steal anything Senator, we are simply making sure that the public money will be used for the public good.

Phylurgus You are aware that the funds in question had been set aside for a national emergency.

Lysistrata The real national emergency is the poverty, depopulation, famine and disease that this war has brought to Greece.

(The women applaud and agree vociferously)

Kalike Yeah, the emergency fund should be used to feed the hungry, to re-establish Greek agriculture, to fight disease, and not to carry on a war from which we'll never recover, even if we do manage to win it.

Demostratus *(to Lysistrata)* Are we to believe that economic considerations are of greater importance to you than the honour of your homeland?

(There is silence as Lysistrata thinks of a retort.)

Lysistrata I– I–

(The police snigger and the women gasp as they think she may be floundering but...)

Lysistrata	Honour is a smokescreen that you've erected to hide the profiteers.

(The women are overjoyed at her clever response)

Nikias	And exactly who are you suggesting is a profiteer?
Lysistrata	The military leaders who increase their personal power and influence. The politicos who are only in power because all the good men are occupied in battle. And businessmen like you.
Police *(turning on Nikias)*	What?
Nikias	This is outrageous!
Lysistrata	That is why we have taken over the Exchequer, Senator. In future *we* will design the Budget.

(The women cheer; the police chant 'Athena!' enthusiastically. Demostratus calms them down)

Lysistrata	Now, Senator Peisander, *(the women boo)* your wartime responsibility is law and order.
Peisander	That is correct and I consider I do a very good job of it...
Women	Rubbish! Bollocks!
Peisander	...in the face of the low morals we see here today. It's people like you who bring chaos to the streets.
Lysistrata	You moan about the chaos in the streets, about the decline in public morality but can't you face the fact that this is simply the result of *your* war.
Iris	Haven't you seen *your* soldiers haunting the brothels, beating up shopkeepers, stabbing each other? *(The police enjoy this idea)*
Myrrhine	Can't you see that they're just bringing home the behaviour that *you* taught them on the battlefield?

(The police stand up and face the women in the audience, protesting, threatening etc. The women give as good as they get. The cleaning women come forward and grab the soldiers and push them to the side.)

Stratyllis   Behave yourselves! I warned you before!

Lysistrata   You blather about the decay of law and order and put it down to every reason but the right one – the war.

Phylurgus   So you ladies are going to save us from ourselves?

Women   Yes! That's right! Somebody's got to!

Phylurgus   That's ridiculous. It's a crime against nature, to put the government into the hands of women.

Lysistrata   War is the greatest crime against nature.

Nikias   Nonsense, it's part of the scheme of things. Animals fight for what they want.

Lysistrata   Since when has our ambition been to live like animals?
(The women applaud and laugh)

Phylurgus   You really are insufferable. A female know-all, there's nothing more repulsive on earth. I ought to conscript the lot of you. *(The women mock this idea)* You seem to think war is some sort of picnic. The enemy aren't the only ones who get hurt!

Police *(butching up and looking proud)* Yeah!

Lysistrata   If it weren't for the war, Senator, you'd have had to give way to younger men long ago. A man like you gives sons to the war without a qualm because you're so besotted with your war philosophy but even you must grow tired of

	carnage. Don't you ever feel doubt or, God forbid, guilt crowding on your soul?
Peisander	And why then do you suppose men are willing to sacrifice their lives?
Police	That's right.
Lysistrata	I don't believe they are willing. Many of them are simply scared because they know that you've ordered these thugs to hunt down and shoot dissenters.

(The police laugh and have fun pretending to shoot and throw grenades at dissenters)

Phylurgus	Your simple-minded pacifism was nauseating enough, but this infantile political theory is truly laughable. Your problem, my dear lady, is simply ignorance. You don't know what you're talking about. *(The police laugh)*
Lysistrata	Oh, I think we know this war pretty well, don't you, ladies?
Women	Yeah!
Lysistrata	No one drugs us with battle songs and flashy uniforms, or with wine and captive women. We just watch and wait. Watch our husbands and sons marching off to nowhere, for no good reason.
Phylurgus	You're young to have a son at the war!
Lysistrata	You know I do not speak for myself but for all the voiceless women who agree with me. If this war goes on much longer I'll never have a son.
Stratyllis *(to Phylurgus)*	I'm getting pretty sick of that smirk on your face, mate. All my kids have got left of their father is an empty place at the table. *(She moves to attack him but the police force her off and she is comforted by Nikodike)*

Kalonike   And you thought no more of our men
                 than to send them to fight.
Praxagora   And what for?
Katina   For six feet of ground in bloody Sicily.
*(The police move away from the Senators, considering
this. The women cheer.)*
Lysistrata   What have you to say to the little
                 sisters? The young girl whose head is
                 filled with dreams... what will you say
                 to her while you send her lover to be
                 massacred or brutalised for policy?
                 Would you have him come home to
                 her, experienced in rape and the mur-
                 der of children, full of the madness and
                 disease of military life, bringing his
                 shame to her bed?
Myrrhine   Why should *you* live? My Kinesias is
                 dead for all I know!
Lysistrata   I think we've wasted enough energy on
                 them for now, don't you? Women, the
                 charge against the Senate is incomp-
                 etence and that they are unfit to
                 govern. Do we find the defendants
                 guilty or not guilty?
Women   Guilty!
Lysistrata   Take them away and think of a suitable
                 punishment for them.
Stratyllis *(to Phylurgus)* You come with us love. We'll
                 sort you out.

*(The Senators are led off through the upstage centre
exit by the cleaning women amidst chants of 'Guilty!'
from the characters in the audience.)*

Lysistrata *(turns to the women/audience)* Women for
                     Peace, it is not our intention to destroy
                     femininity or the softness of women's

nature. The war shall cease because
men admire and desire us. Our gifts are
those that foster life, and in pursuing
the cause of peace we do no more than
is consistent with women's nature. To
seek a military solution to a political
problem is as silly as... as... as if we
women, when we got our threads
caught up in our tapestries were to grab
a sword to slash at the knot. There will
always be great variations in our lands,
like the many wools that give richness
and vividness to our tapestries; differ-
ences in speech, in work, in appear-
ance, but we should rejoice at them,
and not make them a cause for hatred
and bigotry. This is not idealism that I
speak, but a simple law of survival.
*(She turns to the police, lurking at the
back)* Now if you gentlemen will excuse us. We have a Peace to organise.
That is unless you'd like to stand trial.

*(The guards run for it through the audience, taunted by
the women as they go. Demostratus is left behind. The
women don't notice him sat behind a pillar lost in
thought.*

*The Senators are ushered in by the cleaning women.
The men have been forced by the cleaners to swap
clothes with them. The women are dressed in towels for
the steam bath and the men are wearing aprons, head-
scarves and carrying the cleaning equipment. The
society women wolf-whistle and return to the stage to
see these curious male specimens close up.)*

Nikias   This is the worst moment of my life.

Peisander   Ye gods, what an outrage!

Phylurgus   I suppose you'll bring us men to our
knees, force us to do ignoble work,
gird us with aprons instead of swords.

Lysistrata   So! Women's work's ignoble is it?

Kalonike   And to think I nearly believed them
when they said housework was the
foundation of society. Oh doesn't he
look lovely! Just like my old granny.

Peisander   No man who is a man can suffer this
disgusting humiliation.

Nikias   Do you think we will all have to throw
ourselves on our swords?

Stratyllis   No just keep the place spick and span
like we had to. Mop out the latrines,
pick up the dead skin, don't forget the
toenail clippings. You'll get used to it.
(The women laugh)

Katina   Ooh you are a sexy old scrubber!

Lysistrata   I think you've got off quite lightly. So
perhaps you'd like to begin your work,
unless you'd like us to think of a new
punishment.

Stratyllis   Come on, we'll show you what to do.

*(All the women, except Lysistrata, usher the men,
except Demostratus offstage through the centre stage
exit. Lysistrata remains. The stage is finally quiet and
we hear the peaceful sound of crickets. She doesn't
notice Demostratus watching her as she splashes water
from a pool on her face. She suddenly looks tired and
vulnerable.)*

After a while

Demostratus   Of course it's not as simple as you
seem to think. A decisive victory for us
brings peace to all.

Lysistrata   Oh, Demostratus. I'm not arguing that
stopping the war is the only solution to
all the problems caused by the war. But
sending soldiers to a scene of civil un-
rest or international tension just adds
more problems. Suppose the invading
army *can* bombard the various factions
into some kind of agreement, do you
really think those agreements will hold
in the long term? (*Demostratus goes to
leave. She challenges him*) Negotiated
peace is the only solution.

Demostratus *(turning back)* When did you become so
sure of yourself?

*(There is a spark of attraction between them in spite of
their opposing views. They relish this sparring.)*

Lysistrata   During all those long evenings, listening to my father and then my husband
making war from their armchairs. I
knew they were spouting rot and that
somewhere people were dying for it.
Perhaps sometimes I'd say, 'Dear, in
the Assembly today, did you decide
anything about peace?'... 'Look after
your affairs and I'll attend to mine.
Shut up,' he'd say and so I did. Like a
good little woman I held my tongue.
And then I'd hear that the Senate was
for escalation of the war and I'd ask my
respected husband how he could ever
have agreed to something so wicked
and so futile, and he'd frown and
mutter, 'You look after your house-
keeping. War is men's business.'

Demostratus   War *is* men's business. What is it about women that they can't realise when they're well off?

Lysistrata   I couldn't sit quietly any longer. I couldn't sit there and do nothing while whole civilisations butchered each other. I believe in negotiating for peace. That's why I set up a peace treaty with the enemy who are as de-moralised as we are... Oh, with the women of course, just to make you understand that it's only the men who are at war. We women have never declared war on each other in any country ever in history.

Demostratus   Some people would call this treason.

Lysistrata   No, Demostratus – *you* are the traitor. You used your gifts as an orator to persuade the people back into this ruin-ous war which will destroy Greece, if we can't stop it.

Demostratus   Every traitor in history has claimed to be acting for the good of his country. Every sneaking spy cries out he's a pacifist.

Lysistrata   War is what destroys cities. Peace never destroyed a city yet.

Demostratus   You don't think then that the Spartans would destroy us if we were defenceless?

Lysistrata   If we were defenceless, why should they?

Demostratus   So you're for peace at any price?

Lysistrata   No! It's you who are for war at any price. At every level peace costs less.

Demostratus   You don't think your seizure of power was war-like?

Lysistrata	Only because it had to be. We didn't glory in it.
Demostratus	And you think men do?
Lysistrata	I know they do. *(Pause)* The last time I heard from my husband, he was leading an attack on a vital military installation. So, I looked it up on the map. It was a small fishing village. *(We hear the sound of a cannon)* What was that?
Demostratus	Ah ha! I believe that's the tenth battalion firing out to sea to let their women know they're back. A thousand fighting men home for a fortnight's leave. Good luck Lysistrata! You're going to need it.

Lights fade on them.
Music. (Julie London sings 'Mad About the Boy'.)

End of Act.

ACT TWO

The Bathhouse now shows definite signs of the women's occupation. There is female debris everywhere. It's a fun, lively colourful place, soft furnishings, make-up, rubber ducks, used cotton buds, magazines strewn everywhere. There is a washing line with sexy underwear on it, strung between two pillars. Underneath the 'Male Members Only' sign someone has written in lipstick: 'yes please'. The women are onstage playing with beach balls, doing their make up, reading etc.

Stratyllis enters with a pile of bananas on a plate. The women eat them enthusiastically and, in some cases, obscenely. From offstage we hear the sound of a group of soldiers singing: 'Get your tits out for the lads'. The society women scream and run off through centre stage exit. Katina runs with them but is stopped by Nikodike: 'Oh no you don't.' Enter Lysistrata.

Lysistrata	Oh sisters, help me! I can't bear it!
Rhodippe	Nay luv, tell us what's the matter.
Katina	Aw, c'mon, man, you mus'na lose heart now.
Lysistrata	It's those damn women. They drive me to despair.
Stratyllis	Nothing that lot would do, would surprise me.
Lysistrata	They gave me so much grief that I organised self-defence training sessions – and the belly-dancing classes they wanted, everything, make-up and beauty! But they're all trying to escape! They go parading by the windows in flimsy dresses, dropping rude notes to the passing soldiers. One little sneak tried to dig her way out through the cellar. Another ruined half a dozen sheets trying to make a ladder.
Nikodike	Silly bitch.
Lysistrata	I came across one girl letting herself out the front door as cool as you please. They bitch and bicker all day long like spoiled children. I don't understand... Why can't they treat each other decently? I can't get them to show hostility to the men and I can't get them to stop showing it to each other. It's impossible.
Rhodippe	Perhaps it's because they're not used to being with other women.
Stratyllis	They know more about men than they do about each other, I suppose.

Rhodippe	We don't have that problem, do we?
Nikodike	Things are different in the beggars' army!
Stratyllis	So far, touch wood.
Lysistrata	Look at this idiot. *(Kalike is trying to escape by tiptoeing round the back of the stage)* Where on earth are you going?
Kalike	Oh! Lysistrata! I just thought I'd pop home for a minute. I bought some super new wool the other day, you see and I've forgotten to put it in the camphor chest and the moths must already be hopping into it. I combed the city for it for aeons and I couldn't bear to think of it being ruined.
Lysistrata	And it's got absolutely nothing to do with the tenth battalion coming home on leave, has it, darling!
Kalike *(with studied indifference)*	Are they? Oh, I didn't know.
Lysistrata	Well, now you *do* know darling so you understand why your wool will have to wait. It wouldn't be moths munching your wool if you went home now, would it?

(The cleaning women laugh raucously)

Kalike	I only wanted to see it nicely spread out in the chest.
Lysistrata	I really can't spare anyone to see you don't find yourself nicely spread out.
Kalike	Oh Lysistrata, you don't trust me! *(She throws herself onto the floor and beats it in exaggerated grief)* all my lovely wool ruined... ruined... ruined...

Nikodike   Never mind blossom, you'll find
                      somebody to look after your pretty
                      wool.
Kalike   What do you mean?
Stratyllis *(suggestively prodding her)* One of those
                      Spartan gals'll give it a bit of a poke
                      and a stroke.
Kalike   Oooh! Common women! *(Runs to a*
                      corner and sulks)

(The cleaning women roar with laughter. Iris pops up
through a trapdoor right in front of Lysistrata. She has
obviously been spotted so decides to face it out:)

Iris   Oh Lysistrata! How nice! I was just
                      looking for you!
Lysistrata   What can I do for you?
Iris *(as she walks past the cleaning women she notices*
                      they smell really strongly) I was about
                      to ask... if – if I could... I managed to
                      get some marvellous flax you see, good
                      as pre-war stuff, on the black market
                      and I thought –
Lysistrata   And what happened then?
Iris   I thought I might just slip home and
                      get it stripped before it spoils.
Lysistrata   Even if I believed you, aren't you ash-
                      amed to have your heart set on such
                      trifles?
Iris   I just wanted to get it stripped, just a
                      half hour and I'd be back again.
Rhodippe   Let Nikodike do it for you. She'll have
                      it stripped to the bone for you in
                      seconds.
Iris   What, her?
(Nikodike chases her round the stage, barking like a
small dog. Iris also finds a corner to sulk in.)

Stratyllis	*(laughing)* I wonder what it'll be next? *(crudely and suggestively)* Their puddings stirring?
Nikodike	Their rugs beating?
Katina	Their chicken stuffing?
Rhodippe	Their eel jellied?
Nikodike	I'll just run along and glaze my meat-loaf...

(Praxagora staggers through the centre entrance clutching the wine bowl from Act One to her stomach under her towel and making a great show of having labour pains.)

Praxagora Oh Hecate, patroness of childbirth, stay my infant's coming till I reach my own bed. Oh Lysistrata, my baby has decided to come... My pains are coming regularly. I'll have to get home.

(Praxagora moves out into the auditorium to escape but is stopped by Lampito who is suddenly blocking her way.)

Lampito Got a problem, Lysistrata?

Lysistrata Bless you, darling, but I think now that women are in control, you can have your jolly baby here. (*Praxagora is retrieved from the auditorium by the cleaning women and pushed down on the floor*) Legs apart dear.

(The cleaning women cradle her knees and feet.)

Praxagora Without a midwife! Lysistrata, do you want to kill me?

Rhodippe Who needs a midwife? I had my five on a farm in the mountains while my husband cowered in the kitchen. We'll be your midwives dear... Hold my hand when the pain gets bad.

Stratyllis	Come on, mi'lady, knees up for a little push.
All	Push!

(Rhodippe reveals the bowl which has been dislodged by the women. She smacks its bottom.)

Rhodippe	My, that's a good heavy infant.
Lysistrata	You awful cheat.
Praxagora	Well, the idea was to use the bowl to carry the baby in if I did ever get pregnant.
Stratyllis	There's no danger of that if you stay put.
Lysistrata	Stop this nonsense, I'm ashamed of you.
Praxagora	Oh Lysistrata, you're a hard woman.

(She also sits down to sulk. Kalonike enters upstage centre wearing a headscarf and Jackie O' type dark glasses. She sweeps down the stage and into the auditorium.)

Kalonike	Bye, darlings, lovely to meet you. Let's do lunch soon, sweetheart.
Lysistrata	Kalonike!
Kalonike	I'm sorry, darling, but I can't make it.
Lysistrata	Even you, my oldest friend. What about your oath?
Kalonike	It's not that I want to sleep with my husband. I just want to sleep. *(Not realising Lampito is standing directly behind her in the auditorium)* Those blasted Spartan women keep me awake every night singing dirty songs. *(She turns and sees Lampito and gives a little scream, then moves onto the stage to show Lysistrata the bags*

under her eyes behind the glasses) I'm ragged darling, simply ragged.

Lysistrata You should have asked me sooner; I'd have changed your sleeping quarters, given you earplugs but I will not let you go. *(A chorus of cries breaks out.)*

Kalonike Please, let us go!

Kalike You can't keep us!

Praxagora It's against the law!

Iris It's kidnapping!

Kalonike Don't you know when you're beaten?

Lysistrata Women, women... I know you've had a hard time. But you can't give up now. I know the tenth battalion are on home leave *(the society women all sigh longingly)* but this is what it's all about. Now is the time they have got to find out that their loving wives are not putting out. If we didn't want them anyway there wouldn't be any point. *(The cleaning women all move in on the society women to comfort them)* It's because we want them that we won't let ourselves have them until the war is over. Then maybe we'll get our men back in one piece. Living with them like man and wife again. Don't you see? You can't make love and war. Peace with love, or war without. That's the bargain and we've got to stay with it until it's driven. But I will not make any woman stay here against her will.

(A beat. Then all the society women make a mad scramble to leave through the auditorium. The cleaning women groan with frustration. In desperation to do anything to stop them Lysistrata says:)

Lysistrata	I've consulted the Oracle!
	(The women stop)
Women	Oh!
Lysistrata	This morning early, I offered a prayer for guidance. Of course as you know I have been continent, and I was fasting– *(she is temporising and building up suspense)* ...and I was given the grace of an Oracle.
Kalike	Oh, Lysistrata – how marvellous!

(The society women return to the stage and crowd around Lysistrata. Myrrhine enters from upstage centre to hear what she has to say, followed by the Senators still in their charwomen clothes and carrying cleaning equipment.)

Stratyllis	*(to the other cleaning women)* Oracle, my arse!
Iris	How did you get it?
Praxagora	Did you hear the voice of Zeus?
Lysistrata	Er, no. Writing appeared on a wax tablet.
Iris	How perfectly smashing!
Kalonike	Funny, I've tried lots of times and never got a peep out of it.
Kalike	Go on, Lysistrata. What did it say?
Lysistrata	*(paces, thinking very fast)* What did it say? It said... you are the chosen ones, and must treat each other with love and reverence.
Women	*(very carried away)* Love and reverence.
Iris	Does that mean we can do all those secret rituals and everything?
Lysistrata	All acts of love and tenderness between you are sanctified. There is no need now to be fidgeting and dreaming

of escape. We must elaborate the myst-
eries of the Holy Sisterhood, the secret
graces of the daughters of Bilitis living
in joyful seclusion. You have wonders
to perform...

Women   Wonders!

*(They follow Lysistrata off, carried away by their
enthusiasm)*

Stratyllis   Fuck me, it worked! *(She sees the
Senators)* What are you lot staring at.
Haven't you got work to do?

*(She exits upstage. The Senators get down to some
scrubbing)*

Peisander   I've always thought that if we men had
any sense we'd never get involved with
women.

Phylurgus   They're like a separate race. They don't
look like us, they don't talk like us,
they don't think like us. You should
never let a woman know what you're
up to.

Nikias   My wife's not allowed into my study—
not even to dust it. I won't even tell my
wife how much money I make, much
less how I make it!

Phylurgus *(looking at what he has picked up on his
scrubbing brush)* Sometimes I think
women really disgust me.

(The cleaning women appear at the back unnoticed.)

Peisander   I can't help thinking about that chap,
Melanion.

Nikias	The one who did a runner when he found out he was getting married?
Peisander	Resourceful fella, kept moving around all over Greece, camping out in the woods.
Nikias	Only took his dog and his hunting knife.
Peisander	That I understand. I'm sure my dog likes me a good deal more than my wife does.
Stratyllis	What a touching tale! Wasn't he lucky though, to get away!
Nikodike	Women don't find it so easy to get away camping for a lifetime!
Katina	My mum was married at fourteen and her husband was fifty. Tried to kill herself after the wedding night… she survived though.
Rhodippe	Little girl in our town died in child-birth because she wasn't fully-grown.
Nikodike	Some bastard hid in the bushes by our cowshed and frightened the life out of my little sister when she was only a tot.
Rhodippe	You never hear of women doing things like that to men!
Katina	The soldiers like to rape the farm girls when they come by for provisions.
Stratyllis	Oh, I've seen that. The girls would hide in the pigswill, roll themselves in cow shit, but it never put those brutes off.

(Enter Lysistrata upstage centre.)

Lysistrata	Ye Gods, this is all I need!
Nikodike	Now what?
Stratyllis	More trouble in the ranks?

Lysistrata	Perhaps! There's a man and he's heading this way.
Rhodippe	Nay, love, there are men everywhere.
Lysistrata	Not like this one. This is the genuine article. He's only half way up the hill but you can clearly see his credentials.
Stratyllis	You mean you, can see it from there? Bloody Hell!

(Kalonike, Iris, Praxagora, Lampito and Kalike appear behind Lysistrata.)

Kalonike	Yummy! Lysistrata, have you seen what's heading our way?
Lysistrata *(wearily)*	Yes, I have.
Kalonike	Do you suppose he's delivering that package here? *(Dirty laugh)*
Lysistrata	That path doesn't lead anywhere else.
Kalonike	What gorgeous lumpy thighs! *(Myrrhine enters and overhears)* Do you suppose we could take him prisoner?
Lysistrata	A prisoner of love and peace. *(Laughs)*
Kalonike	We could bind him hand and foot and beat him with silk scarves, I suppose. *(Girly giggles of anticipation)*
Myrrhine	Why don't you just stand him in the courtyard and play quoits?
Lysistrata	Do we know him?
Myrrhine	I suppose I do. That's my husband, Kinesias, in all his glory.
Kalonike	Is he always like that?
Myrrhine	Pretty much. It depends what underpants he's wearing, what he had for lunch, how long since he's had it, that kind of thing.

Lysistrata *(blows a whistle on a string of pearls around her neck)* Right-o, girls, this is our chance. *(to the Senators)* Boys, make yourselves scarce. *(to the women)* Girls, places please, you know what you've got to do. (*Lampito and Kalonike put lipstick on Myrrhine. Lysistrata turns to Rhodippe)* You meet him at the door. Get him out of his uniform and into a towel.

(Rhodippe exits through the auditorium.)

Myrrhine Will I do?

Lysistrata You would if you could, I don't doubt. Now you can do anything you like but you must stop short at the critical moment, understand. Lead him on, let him touch you, let him see your body but don't put your hand on his, um… accoutrements – you could ruin everything.

Myrrhine Lysistrata, I don't like it!

Rhodippe *(from back of auditorium)* Here she is!

(Rhodippe leads Kinesias to a vantage point in the audience. His erection is very prominent beneath his towel. The women present Myrrhine at the centre of a sexy Busby Berkeley style water ballet. A vision of Botticelli's Venus (to the strains of Julie London's 'Call Me Irresponsible'). At the end of the number the women have made a bed out of the benches and formed a tableau around Myrrhine, enticing and making eyes at Kinesias all the time:)

Kinesias Myrrhine, what are you doing here?

Myrrhine It's the Universal Tonguebath.

Kinesias	What on earth is that?
Myrrhine	It's where we lick each other all over. *(The women lick their lips)* It's wonderful, but men aren't allowed, *(The women wag their fingers in a teasing way)* not while they're defiled, anyway. We're going to have a Great Group Grope soon... *(The women all stroke each other)* ...that's a terrifically nice ceremony.
Kinesias	Oh Myrrhine, I've missed you so. I'm bursting with love for you. Look darling, all for you. *(His rigid penis lifting his towel)*

(The women scream with delight)

Lysistrata	Welcome to the bathhouse. If I may explain the rules of the establishment.
Kinesias	There! I knew it was a brothel! *(The women bridle)* My wife is not staying here!
Myrrhine	How dare you call me a whore!
Kinesias	I didn't, I said this was a brothel and so it is!
Myrrhine	And I'm here under my own free will.
Kinesias	Dear god! Why?
Lysistrata	We have renounced the company of men, until peace is declared in the Peloponnesian countries. To this end we have set up headquarters here, we have occupied the Acropolis and sequestrated the emergency funds.

(The women do the 'Women for Peace' sign.)

Kinesias	A political brothel! That's worse! Myrrhine, my goddess wife, come home with me! I've brought you such pretty things from Sicily, look – *(he*

	takes a shell bracelet out of his kit bag and holds it out to her enticingly)
Myrrhine	Ooh, shells! *(She moves to leave the stage and go to him)*
Kinesias	There's more at home, don't you want to come?
Iris	Of course she wants to come!
Praxagora	She never sees a cucumber but she sighs for her Kinesias. *(All sigh)*
Kalike	Never peels a banana but she murmurs your name. *(They all murmur)*
Katina	Now that we have seen you, we can quite understand her obsession.
Kinesias	Would you mind awfully all going away? I have things to discuss with my wife.
Lysistrata	Well, if we're cramping your style...
Lampito	We won't be far away, Myrrhine. Yell if you need us. *(She winks)*

(The women exit but linger in upstage centre doorway, hoping to see the action)

Lysistrata *(offstage, blows her whistle)* Girls!

(The women reluctantly leave. Kinesias moves up to his wife who moves away. The whole speech is delivered as he pads around behind her, trying to get closer.)

Kinesias	Oh darling, I long to hold you. You'll never know how many nights I dreamed of you... what wonderful dirty things you did in my dreams. When I got home, I'd been thinking about you so much I already had this – *(indicating his erection)* I went rushing in like a bull at a gate. And you weren't

there. I hunted everywhere. I thought
you might be in the bath and such
wonderful ideas came into my head.
Then I thought you might have been
taking a nap and I plotted the nicest
way to wake you up. I ran round the
garden like a billy goat. Then the nurse
told me you hadn't been home for a
while. Oh, Myrrhine, the house was
suddenly as dark and cold as a tomb.
Oh my fascinating little wife, I love
you so!

Myrrhine *(wavering)* Oh Kinesias! *(Pulling herself
together)* Stop it! You don't really want
me, you just want *it*.

Kinesias No, Myrrhine, no! No other woman in
the world excites me the way you do.

Myrrhine So you've had all the other women in
the world have you?

Kinesias No... would I be running round like a
ram in rut if I had? *(He deliberately
bangs her with his phallus)*

Myrrhine Kinesias! How can you? *(She puts one
finger on his phallus and elaborately
walks round it)* You're so insensitive to
a woman's needs. You rush in here
with Mr Wibbly on end and expect me
to fling myself down and serve you!

Kinesias Don't you want it? Don't you want it
just a little bit?

Myrrhine I've been worrying about you since the
day you left. I have terrible dreams of
you lying disembowelled on the battle-
field or running wild with the other
soldiers, killing children and raping
women like a maniac. I'm frightened
that you've turned into a monster.

Kinesias   Officers don't get to do much raping,
or killing either for that matter. I'm still
as soft as butter.

Myrrhine   That's not how you look to me.

Kinesias   Sweetheart, if I've been too sudden for
you, I'll try to control myself. I'll do
whatever you want. Just tell me what it
is, that's all…I can't behave naturally
in this mad place. I'm on the defensive
all the time. I'm sure those crazy
women are peering at me. *(He looks
round the doorway upstage centre and
is greeted by a scream reminiscent of
an audience at a boy band concert)*
Come home with me and we'll have a
bath together and a roll in the big bed.

Myrrhine *(nearly follows him off but retains her
resolve)* I can't. I can't.

Kinesias   Don't you even want to come home
and play with the baby? *(She glares at
him)* He misses you too, love,
probably more than I do.

Myrrhine *(furious)* Oh you are the end! Using the poor
baby to get your way with me. I know
what you're after, you big fat pig! But I
can't come home… I promised.

Kinesias   Right, then we'll do it here!

Myrrhine   How would you like it, standing up
like animals or grovelling on the floor?

Kinesias   Actually I don't think I could manage a
knee-trembler.

Myrrhine *(pretending to soften)* I think we can do
better then that.

Kinesias   That's my girl. I knew you really loved
me. You're prettier than when I left,
you know that? Motherhood suits you.

Myrrhine   Are you saying I'm fat?

Kinesias	No, no, not at all. You're still the same saucy, teasing, childlike little darling I left behind. *(He begins rubbing his phallus rhythmically against her thigh)* What's my baby love doing in this howwible place wif all these frightful women, hmmm? Doesn't my cheeky-bot want to come home?
Myrrhine	Stop treating me like a child!
Kinesias	You used to like that game.
Myrrhine	Not any more. It makes me sick!
Kinesias	Good! That's a relief. You used to make me play it for days on end.
Myrrhine	I've grown up a bit since then. I'm trying to develop some sort of person-ality, you know, thoughts of my own.
Kinesias	Your own or the sisterhood's?
Myrrhine	Mine. I've been thinking, Kinesias. *(She sits him down on the 'bed')* For many years now, the war–
Kinesias *(pushing her back on the bed)*	Mmm, yes, darling. Oh, you smell lovely, what have you got on your hair? *(Myrrhine falls back on the bench, but quickly rolls off it backwards, leaving him floundering)*
Myrrhine	You inconsiderate brute. It's alright for you, bouncing around on top of me, but don't you think I'd have more chance of enjoying it if the bare boards weren't hurting my back?
Kinesias	Sorry dear. I guess I'm a bit impatient. You can understand that, can't you? I've been like this for hours. Soon I won't be able to do it– I'll be on high forever! Please don't play with me.

Myrrhine   Me? Play with you? You're the one
who sweeps in here all ready for his
game. I'm supposed to be sitting in the
toy-box waiting for you to come and
bash my head on the floor.

Kinesias   Can't we find a mattress somewhere?

Myrrhine   Oh darling! You only had to ask!

*(The cleaning women bring on a mattress and throw it
on top of him, amid sniggers)*

Kinesias   Bloody women. How can you abandon
your own child and your nice home for
this nunnery? I swear they're all
touched. *(A burst of giggling offstage)*

Myrrhine   You look a bit of a silly billy yourself,
standing there like a hat stand.

Kinesias   Well it's your fault, you tease!

Myrrhine *(lying provocatively on the mattress)* Why
do you men always blame us for it?
You were in that condition long before
you even saw me.

Kinesias   No, it *is* you... those little titties peep-
ing out... those wicked little curls
trying to creep in your ears... the way
you wag that maddening little bum.

Myrrhine *(gets up)* I want a pillow.

Kinesias *(really turned on)* Oh marvellous, she wants a
pillow. Where will you put it, you sexy
beast? Give us a kiss, go on.

Myrrhine   I don't mind if I do.
(She kisses his forehead)

Kinesias   I mean a real kiss.

*(He plunges, she evades. The pillow arrives, brought by
one of the cleaning women who presents it elaborately)*

Kinesias *(turned on by the sight of her bottom sticking
out as she plumps the pillow)* Let's
have a look at you. I want to see all of
you as naked as the gods intended.

Myrrhine *(standing on the bed)* I suppose you want to check off my good points.

Kinesias   I worship you. I never in my life saw anything more beautiful than my wife's body. Let's have a look! *(Myrrhine lifts her towel a little and pirouettes on the bed, then absent-mindedly lets the towel drop as she flicks her hair)* Why do you let it drop just when you get to the exciting part?

Myrrhine   Shall we get some more pillows? *(The cleaning women throw a heap of pillows on Kinesias)*

Kinesias   Myrrhine, what's wrong now? Please come to bed. I want to hold you in my arms and feel you so close to—

Myrrhine   I know what you want to do. I was thinking, I'm going to need some ointment.

Kinesias   What *ointment?* What *for?*

Myrrhine   Don't yell at me! Bawling in my face, that makes me feel *very* sexy, I must say! I tell you I need some ointment and I'm going to have it and if you loved me at all you'd be happy to wait. All you think of is yourself – you wouldn't care how much it hurts me, oh no! *(The ointment is brought by one of the cleaning women)* Here – we'll put some on you too. *(She stands in front of him, his back is to the audience. She appears to be rubbing ointment on his erection. Just before he climaxes she suddenly stops)* Ooops! It's the wrong stuff! This isn't what I meant! Whew, that was a narrow escape!

(Myrrhine exits upstage centre to get some more ointment.)

Kinesias   What do you mean, wrong stuff? I
                      don't need any stuff at all. Myrrhine,
                      you're killing me! Please stop fooling.
Myrrhine *(offstage)* Be patient just a little longer,
                      darling. *(She re-enters and gets back
                      on the bed)* Here, sweetheart, put a
                      dollop of this on! *(She holds out the
                      pot, Kinesias flings it against the wall)*
Kinesias   That's enough, enough, enough! *(He
                      forces her down on the bed)* You heart-
                      less little cock-teaser, you asked for it!
Myrrhine *(struggling)* Just let me get my shoes off!

(The cleaning women and the Senators enter unnoticed at the back.)

Kinesias   Why? They're not in my way.
(Myrrhine brings her knee up sharply to untie her shoe, it catches him in the groin. He collapses and she tears herself away.)
Myrrhine *(genuinely)* I'm sorry.

(The cleaning women have closed ranks and she slips through the centre stage exit. Lysistrata appears in her place.)

Lysistrata   And that's the last you'll see of it, until
                      peace is declared in the Peleponnesus,
                      I'm afraid.
Kinesias   You bitch! What gives you the right to
                      come between a man and his wife?

(Lysistrata ignores him and leaves, indicating to the Senators to carry on cleaning. They begin to clear the

stage of the pillows, mattress, ointment etc. When they have finished, they exit. Peisander remains.)

Kinesias *(to the cleaning women)* I've seen some sinister things in my time, but this sort of white slavery is something new. Go on you – can you speak? What enemy pimps have been hanging around here? How do you old bags get your kicks? What dirty things have you been doing to my wife? God, I can just imagine!... You're disgusting. I can smell your dirty bodies from here... *(to Peisander, not realising he is a man as he is still dressed in his cleaning clothes)* Butch Dykes! Freaks! *(Peisander exits)* Eating yourselves up with jealousy of the happiness of pretty women! We've had some crazy cults in Athens but this disgusting Lesbian brothel takes the bloody bun. *(The cleaning women gaze at him with sad impassivity. He suddenly grabs Katina)* Hey you!... come and help nurse my baby. How'd you like that – clean sheets for the first time in your life? If you behave, you might get eight inches of the best for a bonus! *(Katina is paralysed by terror. The others move in and free her, knocking Kinesias to the ground.)*

Stratyllis Put her down. Don't you think you're a bit confused, lad? Your wife is just trying to strike a bargain with you. She's using the only power she's got – the only power you let her have.

Rhodippe	And that wouldn't be much without us old bags putting a bit of brawn behind it.
Nikodike	As long as we're good and do as we're told, we're the prettiest, cutest little things on legs, but the minute we show a will of our own, no abuse is too bad for us.

(The women leave him on the floor and move to put the benches back to where they were before the 'bed'. The Senators appear through one of the trap doors next to Kinesias.)

Phylurgus	We could have told you about that Myrrhine.
Peisander	She's a tart, a cold, hard, ambitious tart.
Nikias	She was always flaunting her skimpy charms and ogling me.
Phylurgus	You might as well leave her in this bizarre whorehouse.
Peisander	All women are pestilent pus bags.
Nikias	Done-up in tarty dresses and perfumes and swags of hair.
Peisander	You forget it lad. Why buy a book when you can join a library?
Kinesias *(in great distress)*	It's not true! I love Myrrhine. I'm obsessed by her. *(His loud protestations attract the attention of the cleaning women)* Her body is my joy, better than nectar or ambrosia. I love to smell her on my fingers! I don't even mind having to breathe through her hair in bed. Everything about her delights me!
Phylurgus	But she's like a peach, new-plucked…

Peisander	A fish new-caught in its bright scales. Your kitten will become a cat.
Nikias	Your chicken will grow into a fowl.
Peisander	Her firmness will sag, her brightness dim.
Phylurgus	Her sweet breath turn sour and her soft voice harsh.
Nikias	Then you'll discover that she has the mind of a flea and the heart of a toad, spitting poison continually.

(The cleaning women have come up behind the Senators and surprise them. They resume cleaning hurriedly.)

Stratyllis	Don't let yourself listen to their lies, boy. You mustn't let them destroy your happiness. Myrrhine will make you happy again, if you respect her terms.
Kinesias	I don't understand. What terms? What am I supposed to do?
Stratyllis	We must have peace. We get peace and you'll get your oats.
Kinesias	But what can I do? Does Myrrhine imagine that I waltzed off to war of my own free will?
Nikodike	This is the only way she can make you realise how determined she is. She's running a terrible risk you know. I bet she's crying her eyes out somewhere, worried she's lost you for good. But the only way she can get things changed is through you.
Kinesias	But for heaven's sake denying a fellow his conjugal rights – it's blackmail.
Rhodippe	If that's what you want to call it. But she's doing all this because if she

	doesn't act now there will be no world for her son to grow up in.
Kinesias	Do you believe that?
Stratyllis	It's worse than that. Nobody's working on the farms. If this war doesn't stop, anyone who hasn't died in the fighting will soon be dead of starvation.
Katina	They say that disease is spreading from the battlefields. We're fighting for our lives.
Kinesias	But we can't just give in because things have got too tough.
Stratyllis	If you could sit down with the Spartans and the Boetians, as we have, you'd know that things are as bad for them as they are for us. The war itself is every-one's enemy. We should all unite against it.
Kinesias	But that's treachery. Collusion. Con-spiracy. I'm scared –a bloody sight more than I ever was in battle. You know what the penalties are for treason?
Nikodike	And if we don't succeed, your Myrrhine will have to pay them.
Stratyllis	You could start a veteran's movement.
Katina	Aye. Send back your medals and lead an officers' revolt!
Stratyllis	Go on, son, you've got work to do. Get your mates together and have a go.
Kinesias	I daren't do it on my own. I doubt if I can persuade the other officers to join me.
Nikodike	They're all in the same boat, remember! – 'No peace, no sex!'
Rhodippe	You will try, won't you?

Kinesias *(bravely with a little salute)* For love of mad Myrrhine – yes, I'll try.
(He exits through the auditorium)

Phylurgus Boy! Come back here! Don't believe them, they're all liars!

Rhodippe Did you hear us say one thing that wasn't true?

Phylurgus Great nations do not exist on small-minded truths like yours.

Peisander We're a nation of heroes. What are you trying to reduce us to?

Nikias When did you ever hear of a hero in peace time?

Stratyllis A man who could cure the plague or teach the poor to read, or lessen the back-breaking work we face everyday, would be a hero to me. Not some shit-head who herds us into pointless battles.

Phylurgus I suppose you'd rub out the magnificent military history of Greece, and have future generations think of us as a pathetic bunch of freethinkers?

Nikias Isn't that just like a woman, always taking the side of the weirdo?

(The Senators move off into a conspiratorial huddle)

Peisander I used to know a hunchback had more women than he knew what to do with, always hanging around him, sneaking into his house during the night. Society too. You'd be surprised.

Nikias I knew of a peasant girl used to have it away with her pig.

Peisander Oh, come now, that's not on. A pig's got a cork-screw one.

Nikias There are some places where you can watch a girl with a donkey.

Peisander	But that would kill an ordinary woman.
Phylurgus	Well, they use prisoners of war so who's going to object? Used to go myself, now and then.
Peisander	Sounds like a damn good night's entertainment!

(The Senators suddenly notice the cleaners glaring dangerously at them and they clatter off with their mops and buckets.)

Katina	Do you think Lysistrata's plan's worked?
Stratyllis	Sort of. I'm not sure our talking-to didn't do more good than the striptease show in the end.
Rhodippe	You didn't like that prick-teasing business, did you?
Stratyllis	No.
Nikodike	I can't say I go for it much either.
Rhodippe	If there was the slightest chance of seeing my poor old man on his road home, I don't think I'd have the heart to carry on like that.
Nikodike	It's all very well for a floozy like her.
Rhodippe	Oh I dunno. I think I look pretty fetching in this outfit.

(She strikes an attitude. Everyone laughs. Demostratus leads the Spartan Herald through the audience to the stage. The Herald has a huge erection under his towel.)

Demostratus	This bathhouse is the headquarters of 'Women For Peace'. Sorry about the towel. House rules I'm afraid.
Stratyllis	Well now, what's this here then?
Rhodippe	Well, he's a Spartan – that's not hard to see.

Katina	There's something else that stands out too.
Stratyllis	You're in a pretty bad way, wouldn't you say Spartan, hey? What does he look like now?

(They are teasing him, circling him and pushing him down onto a bench.)

Nikodike	A rhinoceros.
Katina	A pole-vaulter.
Rhodippe	A teapot.
Nikodike	There must be a law against it. Lewd and obscene display, wouldn't you call it?
Herald *(trying hard to disguise his erection)*	Well, I'm very sorry but some battle-axe at the door took my clothes and gave me this towel to wear.
Stratyllis	It doesn't leave much to the imagination.
Nikodike	The soldier's simply standing to attention. At ease, lad.
Stratyllis	Down Bonzo, at once.
Herald	Do you mind? I think you're being unnecessarily coarse. What do you expect when I've got to walk past a crowd of ogling girls?
Demostratus	Stop bullying him, why don't you. He's here on official business.
Herald *(moving away)*	I'm a Herald from Sparta, here to negotiate. I've been told this is where I can find Lysistrata.
Rhodippe	I suppose that's your message for Athens. *(pointing)*
Herald	No. It's a spear to ram down your gullet.

(Stratyllis moves in and grabs his erection through the towel. The Herald winces.)

Stratyllis   Now you be a good boy. Nice and
                        respectful if you know what's good for
                        you.

Herald   I'm sorry. *(She lets him go)* But if you
                        will keep embarrassing me so. You've
                        no idea what tortures our Spartan
                        women have been inflicting on us.

Demostratus   What's happened?

Herald   Well, they say they've made a treaty
                        with the women of Athens not to have
                        anything to do with us men until a
                        peace is signed between our countries.
                        It's been terrible. They swing around
                        the streets in flimsy tunics with their
                        hair flowing, and then if you try to talk
                        to any of them or turn to follow one –
                        Bam! you get your teeth bashed in. But
                        it's not just that! Although it is a bit
                        hard that men who haven't seen a
                        decent, healthy bint in months, can't
                        get near enough even to speak to them.
                        It's not just the young blades are gett-
                        ing the treatment. The married men say
                        it's worse... *(He begins unconsciously
                        masturbating his peace treaty scroll
                        faster and faster as this speech goes
                        through)*... their wives are drifting
                        round the house in next to nothing,
                        squirting themselves with perfume and
                        oiling their bodies, and when their law-
                        ful spouses try to get a bit, they're off
                        and away, screaming blue murder. The
                        whole town's gripped by an epidemic
                        of lover's balls. It's not funny any
                        more.

Demostratus   So what's been your counter-strategy?

Herald	We've capitulated, I'm afraid. *(The women gasp)* That's what I'm here for.
Demostratus	What can we do to help you?
Herald	Well... *(the cleaning women crane forward, the Senators appear in the doorway)* They say that if we make peace, they'll be nice, obliging girls again.
Demostratus	So you've come with proposals for peace talks?
Herald	In a word, yes. *(The women cheer)*
Demostratus	She did it! Her ridiculous far-fetched plan worked!
Herald	Who did it?
Women	Lysistrata!
Herald	Oh. It was Lampito organised it all in Sparta. She's one of those great healthy girls that could represent Sparta in the decathlon, you know the sort. Well, she sent word to a bunch of horsy types like herself. I bet they'd work a man up into a fine state, such good, firm seats they've got... Brave men broke down and sobbed in front of everyone.
Phylurgus	You might as well know that it has been nearly as bad here.
Herald *(shocked, as he registers the Senators all standing there in women's cleaning clothes)*	But I thought you were all – *(droops his wrist)* – in Athens, Plato and all that, don't you know.
Phylurgus	See here lad... *(The Senators all butch up and clear their throats in a manly way, handing their brushes back to the cleaning women)* ... the only time my rear orifice was threatened was when I was Ambassador to Sparta. Those

> Spartan Attachés pinched my bum
> black and blue – so we'll have less
> cheap cracks about the sexual practices
> of the Athenians, if you don't mind.
> We're in exactly the same state as you
> *(with a glance at the Herald's phallus)*
> – well perhaps not exactly the same
> state.

Demostratus   To prove it, we'll institute proceedings
for immediate peace talks.

Herald   Here's the written peace proposal from
our side. We'd be happy to have yours
as soon as possible. *(He hands over his
letter stick)* It's peace, peace at last. I'm
off to give the good news. Who knows,
I might get a bit at last! *(He bumps his
phallus playfully into one of the
Senators as he exits singing:* 'Peace
release me, let me go…')

Women *(taking up the song)* …For he can't stand it
any more… *(Much laughter)*

Phylurgus   Peace, and I can't say I'm sorry.

Peisander *(admiringly)* I don't believe there's anything
more implacable or more merciless in
the world, than a woman.

Demostratus   Did you know that only the female lion
does the killing? The females in the
pride kill for the male.

Nikias   Ever seen a praying mantis eating her
mate– starts at the head and works
down. She's all woman.

Phylurgus   It's a woman's world all right. We are
just their tools, their playthings.

Stratyllis   So why don't you give in gracefully?

(Nikodike exits)

Rhodippe	Why don't you stop scowling and give us a little smile?
Katina	Come on, you silly old billies, make the most of it.
Stratyllis	Shake on it, and let's be friends.
Phylurgus	Friends? And let you in here permanently? Into our pockets?
Nikias	Minds?
Peisander	Lavatories? Never! Women take too long.

Nikodike *(returns with a tray of tea and biscuits)*
Who'd like a little something comforting to warm his drooping spirits?

(Rhodippe takes a cup and biscuit to Peisander and leads him to a bench, Nikodike to Nikias, Stratyllis to Phylurgus. They cuddle and cosset the men. These little scenes are happening almost simultaneously.)

Rhodippe	Feel better now?
Nikias	I feel like I used to when I was a little shaver. Ha ha! .
Peisander	You know you're a bit like a nanny I used to have? How I used to tease her by skipping off in the altogether while she was testing the bath water. Lord, we used to have some fun!.. Mind you I was twenty-five.
Phylurgus	What a big warm soft lap you've got! Wasn't I rude, I only did it to be naughty.
Stratyllis	Now you look human, a proper little man, let's have no more snubs and jeers.

Rhodippe *(to Nikias)* And no more temper tantrums from you, young man.

Katina	Away, Demostratus man, don't look so huffy. Wouldn't you like a bicky too?

Demostratus   I must say they do smell rather good.
                  (He sits down with Katina at his side)
Phylurgus *(putting his barefoot in Stratyllis' lap)* My
                  new sandals rub.
Nikias   I've had a stomach ache, ever since I
                  ate that meatball off the stall in the
                  market.
Stratyllis   Come, come, where does it hurt? Tsk,
                  tsk, is that where your sandal rubbed?
Rhodippe   You need a bit of home cooking,
                  you've got a dicky tummy!
Katina   You're not getting a cold are you?
                  Come now, and…
Women   …blow!
*(The Senators blow their noses in unison into hankies
held by the women)*
Rhodippe   Good! Now we'll give you a big kiss!
Senators *(jiggling down the benches away from the
                  women)* No, no! Don't you kiss me!
                  etc.
Stratyllis   Now stop showing off!
*(Smooch! The women give the Senators a big wet
mumsy kiss.)*
Phylurgus   Pox on you women! How is it you
                  always get your way?
Peisander *(reassuming a little dignity)* It's true what
                  the wise man said— we can' t live with
                  you and we can't live without you.
Nikias   You're the plague and the pleasure of
                  our lives.
Stratyllis   So, peace is declared between the
                  sexes?
Demostratus   A truce, eh? We evermore agree to
                  agree. We will do no harm to women,
                  if they will do no harm to us.
Women   You're on!

*(Sound of an elaborate fanfare as the Spartan Ambass-
ador arrives through the audience, led by the Spartan
Herald. The Ambassador greets members of the
audience warmly as he makes his way to the stage. The
people onstage are all cheering and waving little
Athenian and Spartan flags.)*

Demostratus The Spartan Ambassador!

Rhodippe All hail to the flower of Spartan
manhood.

Stratyllis Greetings and welcome, to the bringers
of peace.

Ambassador *(as he arrives and stands on a bench, his
enormous phallus is at eye-level for all
onstage)* Athenian citizens, you have, I
believe, heard at some length *(Stratyllis sniggers)* of the state of affairs in
Sparta. It is not my intention to expat-
iate upon what our earlier emissary has
told you. *(He turns suddenly and
nearly pokes the Herald in the eye with
his erection)*

Herald *(who has been trying to get his attention all
this time)* Will you save it for the
reception committee?

Ambassador Who are those people then?

Herald They're not important.

*(The crowd groans with indignation and disperses.
The fanfare stops and they put the flags away.)*

Nikodike Been having a bad time, have you?

Herald In short, yes.

Katina In short! That's not what it looks like
from here!

Rhodippe Not from where I'm standing either!

Herald Things have been rather hard with us.

Stratyllis Never mind! Relief is at hand.

(Enter Kinesias, still erect, with an Athenian Attaché through the audience.)

Kinesias   Where's Lysistrata? She should be
here! She set this confounded ball
rolling!
Nikias   Which ball?
Rhodippe   Or is it balls?
Ambassador   The problem between our nations –
*(He and Kinesias turn to face each
other, side on to the audience. It
becomes apparent just how much more
well-equipped the Spartan Ambassador
is than Kinesias, much to Kinesias'
chagrin)* ...is that if we don't get things
back under control fast, the whole
system of sexual legislation will
simply collapse. *(All the men are now
obsessed with the Ambassador's
phallus and are copying its every
move)* Why, the entire city of Sparta is
like one of those brothels where you're
only allowed to look at the whores.
There's such pressure been building up,
we've just had to take the matter in
hand. *(The cleaning women burst out
laughing)* Otherwise, we'd have had to
legalise all sorts of unSpartan behaviour. We've got to get all that sex back
into the marriage bed where it belongs!
Kinesias *(Attaché hands him a scroll)* The most unfor-
tunate development in our situation has
just happened. Young lads have joined
forces with the women, liberated themselves, they call it. There's not a rent
boy to be had.

Herald	Have you seen what the girls did to all the statues of Hermes?
Kinesias	The ones at the doors of the Acropolis!
Herald	Lopped their choppers off! *(The men all wince)*
Katina	Chop, chop!
Ambassador	Good grief! I thought Lysistrata was supposed to be a nice girl?
Demostratus	She is. Frightfully nice. Comes from one of our best families.
Herald	Nice girls don't knock the cocks off statues!
Demostratus	Oh she wouldn't have done that. Not personally.
Nikias	I think the girls in the Acropolis needed them for something.

(A beat while everyone onstage thinks about that. Then big reactions from them all, as they realise what Nikias meant.)

Ambassador	I think that's the most disgusting, outrageous, reprehensible –
Herald	Don't carry on now! We're in Athens.
Demostratus	May I present Lysistrata! Finest flower of Athenian womanhood.

(Lights change. Magic/mystic music plays as the scene almost goes into slow motion. The society women enter centre stage but eyes are on Lysistrata as she moves slowly towards the stage through the audience. The text is spoken in hushed, reverential tones – we are hearing their thoughts out loud.)

Ambassador	Peerless woman.
Herald	This is your finest hour.
Phylurgus	Be clement!
Stratyllis	Be stern!
Katina	Be soft-hearted!

Rhodippe	Be careful!
Demostratus	Be conciliatory!
Nikodike	Be unrelenting!
Nikias	Give us a look at your legs!
Stratyllis	Our fate is in your hands!
Demostratus	You hold our destiny in the palm of your little white hand.
Peisander	You are the arbiter and we have agreed to abide by your decision.
Demostratus	In the hope of establishing a permanent peace.
Nikodike	Take care, Lysistrata, our faith is in you!
Lampito	You're making terms for all of us...
Katina	...for our sake, see that they are respected!

(Lights change. Music out. The scene snaps back into real time, the stage is full of bustle and conversation.)

Kalonike	Darling, you've got them all so rattled they'd agree to anything.
Myrrhine	Poor things, they're afraid they'll be tantalised and ridiculed forever if they don't agree to our terms. Doesn't my Kinesias look miserable?
Lysistrata	Women! *(They gather around her)* Arrange these men on either side of me. Just take them by the hand– or anything else you can get hold of, and lead them. Don't mock them now. I think they're already pretty touchy.

(The women arrange the men in a council of peace. This movement accompanied by the mystic music, also takes place in a dream-like state. When they are all in position, the music finishes and Lysistrata continues:)

Lysistrata	Now you must all listen to me. I'm sorry if you feel uncomfortable, being talked to like this by a woman, but just because I am a woman, I am not necessarily stupid. I blame you both equally *(loud protests from all)* and with equal justification for betraying a brotherhood which has existed between you ever since the beginnings of our common culture and religion. You fought beside each other for centuries and now, when all of Greece is menaced by a Barbarian enemy, who would destroy both of us indiscriminately, you pick a foolish quarrel about a colony.
Herald *(aside to the Ambassador)*	I wish my wife had legs like her! What a classy bit of goods she is, isn't she?
Ambassador	Earlier on I think I caught a glimpse of her pussy!
Lysistrata	Spartans! *(They pull themselves together and kneel in front of her)* Is it so long now that you cannot remember how you sent to us for help?
Kinesias	That's absolutely right, Lysistrata. They're a treacherous lot. They're in the wrong, in the wrong.
Lysistrata	Don't imagine that I have any intention of blaming the Spartans as sole aggressors in this war.

(The Athenians come and kneel in front of her, chastised.)

Ambassador *(to the Spartan Herald)* Look, she's got dimpled knees, look, regular dimpled knees! Isn't that something?

Lysistrata	The Athenians too forgot the friend-ship that Sparta showed us in the past.
Ambassador	Oh Lysistrata, you're stupendous! Tell us what you want us to do!
Herald	Don't you love the way she clenches her little fist? And those flashing great eyes! Too much!
Lysistrata	With such ties to bind you, such warm memories of mutual help and brother-hood, how can you turn against each other now? How can you fight to the death, like mad dogs at each other's throats, knowing that neither can ever win? Won't you make peace?
Ambassador	Oh, darling, I thought you'd never ask. Of course we can. As long as –
Kinesias	As long as what?
Ambassador	As long as you let my long ships rock once more on the gentle swell of the harbour ringed by the fragrant pinewoods…
Demostratus	Look here, are you talking about Lysistrata or Greece?
Ambassador	A little bit of both, I think. The choicest bit.
Demostratus	Speak plainly man, what do you want?
Ambassador	Um. Well, Pylos, for one thing.

(A shocked gasp from the assembly)

Kinesias	No chance.
Lysistrata	Don't bicker, boys. Let him have it.
Kinesias	Don't be a fool, woman, what will we do for an outlet on the coast?
Demostratus	Ask for something in return… Echinos, say.

(The men split off into huddles for whispered negot-iations, then emerge with the answer.)

Kinesias	We'd have to stake a claim to that thickly wooded triangular bit between the legs of Megaera.
Ambassador	*(both turned on by this suggestion)* Take it and welcome. I don't know what you'd do with it though! When I'd stripped my land and ploughed it, I'd sow deep in every furrow.
Kinesias	Why don't you spread dung on it while you're at it?

(They begin to fight. Lysistrata separates them.)

Lysistrata	Very well then, if you won't discuss terms in a rational manner, I shall simply call on you to sign the order for a cease-fire. The details of the armistice can be discussed some other time. I hope you know where your allies stand on the cease-fire agreement.
Ambassador	Our allies stand exactly as we do. All they want is what we want, the sweet society of our women.
Kinesias	A warm house, slippers by the fire, the little woman winding our battle-scarred bodies in her arms.
Men	Hear! Hear!

(Demostratus exits upstage centre for the cease-fire document.)

Lysistrata	Hurry up with the signing, and that's what you'll have. When you've done that, you've got time to go and get yourselves spruced up for the little banquet we're scraping together for you, here tonight. It'll be a bit scratchy, but we've got some decent wine,

which might help to make up for the
shortcomings of the food.

*(Demostratus re-enters and holds the cease-fire
document out with reverence.)*

Demostratus   No sooner said than done, Lysistrata.
                    *(All eyes fixed on the cease-fire
                    document as he travels to centre stage
                    with it. He holds it out to be signed.)*
                    Gentlemen.
                    *(Kinesias and the Ambassador sign it,
                    each trying to be the first to finish)*
                    There you have it.
Lysistrata   Girls! They've signed it! The cease-
                    fire! Let the celebrations begin!

*(Huge cheers and rejoicing from everyone as they
clear the stage of benches and any other debris.)*

Kinesias   Myrrhine, little wifie-pooh! Can I
                    weally take you in my arms?
Myrrhine   Oh daddy darling, your cheeky-bot is
                    tewwibly happy! Can we go home
                    soon? *(They kiss)*

(Lysistrata is borne aloft on the Spartans' shoulders.)

Lysistrata   The War is over! *(More cheers)* Dear
                    friends, my heart is too full for many
                    words. Now at last the reign of peace is
                    established and a man may take his
                    wife again in love and confidence.
                    Now is the time to dance for joy and
                    honour the gods who have granted us
                    the grace that made this possible. I
                    pray that they will also vouchsafe to us
                    a world forever free from wars.
All   Hooray!

(On a whistle from Lysistrata everyone freezes in a pose across the back of the stage reminiscent of paintings on Greek vases. Music. Demostratus and Lysistrata alone begin the dance to Marilyn Monroe's 'Do it again'. Various couples dance across the stage disappearing saucily into the inner steam room: Lysistrata and Demostratus, Kinesias and Myrrhine Rhodippe and Peisander with Kalonike and Phylurgus Lampito beckons Stratyllis into the steam, Nikodike dances with Nikias, the Spartan Ambassador with both Kalike and Katina, Iris and the Herald with Praxagora and Dikaiopolis.
All the men now have huge erections including the Senators who are back in towels. At the end of the dance everyone's towels are thrown over the top of the set from backstage, landing onstage. Suddenly we hear:)

A doorman *(offstage)* You clear off out of it.

(Through the centre door the doorman chases the cleaning women onto the stage from the inner sanctum, throwing their bundles of belongings with them. The atmosphere has changed; it is harsh and subdued.)

Nikodike	But we're friends of Lysistrata!
Doorman	I didn't see any peasant women on the guest list.
Katina	Be a sport mate. Turn a blind eye.
Stratyllis	Aw, go on, sunshine, be a devil. What if I tickle your privates for you?
Nikodike	I'll give you a hand.
Doorman	Stand back! My orders are: Senators, Ambassadors and their families only. We're not expecting any more. Nobody said anything about female vagrants being invited. Now move on! You tramps loitering round here, brings

down the tone of the place.
(He shoves Nikodike)

Nikodike Don't push us around, luv. We're members of 'Women for Peace'.

(They all do the 'Women for Peace' sign)

Dikaiopolis Piss off the lot of you or I'll set the dogs on you! *(He goes back into the party. Silence.)*

Katina I'm hungry.

Stratyllis Sleep a bit, pet. It'll pass.

Rhodippe I don't believe Lysistrata noticed them throw us out. She'd have let us stay.

Stratyllis I don't think she ever noticed us.

Katina Surely she knew we were there at the beginning, in the court?

Nikodike How could she have kept order amongst the women without us?

Stratyllis How did she manage anything? How did she get the enemy women to agree, take over the treasury, storm the Acropolis? How come she was never arrested? *(Beat)* Lysistrata is the heroine of Aristophanes' fantasy. *That's* how she won the Acropolis and united the women and defied the Probuli. In real life Athens was destroyed by the war. This has all been an old man's wartime fantasy.

Katina But we're the peasant women of Greece, as real as rocks and stones. Why can't we be in the happy fantasy?

Stratyllis You've got a lot to learn, luv.

Lights fade slowly to black.
Music. (Marilyn Monroe's 'I want to be loved by you').
The end.